WILLIS HALL

The Long and the Short and the Tall

**Introduction and questions by
Maureen Blakesley**

Heinemann Educational Publishers
Halley Court, Jordan Hill, Oxford OX2 8EJ
a division of Reed Educational & Professional Publishing Ltd
OXFORD   MELBOURNE   AUCKLAND
JOHANNESBURG   BLANTYRE   GABORONE
IBADAN   PORTSMOUTH (NH) USA   CHICAGO

First published in 1959
First published in Heinemann's *Hereford Plays* series 1965
First published in the *Heinemann Plays* series 1994
            02 14 13 12 11 10 9

A catalogue record for this book is available from the British Library on request.
ISBN 0 435 23302 5

Cover design by Keith Ponting

Original design by Jeffrey White Creative Associates

Typeset by Taurus Graphics, Kidlington, Oxon

Printed by Clays Ltd, St Ives plc

CONTENTS

PREFACE

In this edition of *The Long and the Short and the Tall*, you will find notes, questions and activities to help in studying the play in class, particularly at GCSE level.

The introduction provides background information on the author, the historical basis to the play and the circumstances and impact of its first production.

The activities at the end of the book range from straightforward *Keeping Track* questions which can be tackled at the end of each act to focus close attention on what is happening in the play, through more detailed work on characters and themes in *Explorations*.

Right at the end of the book is a glossary of war-time slang and other references used in the play, arranged in alphabetical order.

If you are already using the Hereford edition of *The Long and the Short and the Tall*, you will find that the page numbering in the actual playscript is the same, allowing the two editions to be used side by side.

INTRODUCTION

Willis Hall

Willis Hall joined the professional army when he was 17 and his military service took him to the Far East for several years. While there, he began writing – as a script-writer for the Chinese Schools Department of Radio Malaya and also as a reporter for the *Singapore Standard.*

Back in the UK he had his first major success when *The Long and The Short and The Tall* won the *Evening Standard* Best Play of the Year Award, 1958. Renewing a boyhood friendship with Keith Waterhouse, they adapted Waterhouse's novel *Billy Liar* for the theatre. They have since collaborated on plays and musicals, including *Celebration, Say Who You Are, All Things Bright and Beautiful, The Card,* and the adaptation of two Eduardo De Philippo plays: *Saturday, Sunday, Monday* for the National Theatre and *Filumena,* both of which won Play of the Year awards. Their screenplays include *Billy Liar, Whistle Down the Wind* and *A Kind of Loving.*

As a solo writer, Willis Hall has written extensively for the theatre and television. His Granada TV children's series, *The Return of the Antelope,* has been shown in over 60 countries. He is a prolific children's author and his novels about Count Alucard, the vegetarian vampire, are translated into most European languages. He scripted *The Reluctant Dragon,* which won the BAFTA Best Animation Film Award for 1988.

He has a close association with the Crucible Theatre, Sheffield, and his adaptations there include *Jane Eyre, Mansfield Park* and *The Three Musketeers.*

Historical background to the play

The Long and the Short and the Tall takes place in Malaya during the Second World War (1939–1945). In December

1941 Japan attacked the United States naval base at Pearl Harbour. This was followed by a swift series of Japanese victories in the Pacific.

As the Japanese advance continued into Malaya, the British were forced to retreat to Singapore. Singapore is situated at the end of a long peninsula and protected on the landward side by swamp and jungle. In the belief that any attack from the Japanese would come from the sea, the British fortified Singapore with strong defences against a marine attack. When the Japanese forces poured down through the Malayan peninsula to attack Singapore from behind, it was a complete surprise. The British Forces, their heavy weaponry pointing immovably out to sea, were easily defeated. Malaya was occupied by the Japanese until their surrender in 1946.

The army patrol in Willis Hall's play had been sent from a base north of Singapore to discover the movements and strength of the Japanese army as it swept down through the jungle landscape towards Singapore.

The title and the play

The title is taken from a song which was popular during the Second World War. Originally intended as a harmless ditty for civilian consumption, the song achieved much greater popularity when men of the British Armed Forces, serving in the front line, changed the word 'Bless' throughout the song for a four letter obscenity. In its cruder version, the song expressed the bitterness of the fighting men, risking his life daily in a battle zone, for those fortunate enough to have gained 'safe postings' for themselves in non-combat areas.

The Long and the Short and the Tall is a play about war and attitudes to war. It is not an anti-war play. Rather, it shows us the central moral dilemma of war: can you kill a man in cold blood because he is the enemy when you know that he is also a human being like yourself? Willis Hall does not seek to dictate an answer. He raises the moral dilemma through the dramatic tension which arises as the characters respond in different ways to their Japanese prisoner and leaves the audience with an unsettled, deeply disturbing question.

Characters

At the beginning of the play the characters appear to be easily recognisable types: we have a typical Scotsman, Welshman, Tynesider and Cockney. As the play develops, the characters begin to reveal more of themselves through their interactions with each other and through stories of home and the past.

Mitchem is the sergeant in charge of the patrol. He has a natural authority which is first shown when he discovers Macleish and Bamforth about to fight and restores order quickly. He controls Bamforth by using the sort of sarcasm Bamforth uses on everybody else:

> I've met your kind before. I've seen men who'd make a breakfast out of muck like you go in the nick and do their time and come back so that butter wouldn't melt between their crutch. Don't try and come the hardcase stuff with me, son. It doesn't work. I'm up to all them tricks myself. O.K.

Mitchem's job is to make sure all his men do their duty and to keep them calm and motivated. When the men hear the Japanese on the radio he calms them by attacking their fear ('You've heard one slimy Nippo on the set and now you're having second thoughts') then giving them brisk, specific instructions.

Mitchem's attitude to the war is cynical, realistic and logical. He doesn't like what he has to do but as leader of the patrol he has to make a choice between killing the Japanese prisoner and putting his men in danger. Whatever he thinks and feels personally ('It stinks to me to do for him. Come to that, the whole lot stinks to me!), he uses cold logic to keep emotion out of his decision: 'It's a war. It's something in uniform and it's a different shade to mine'.

Johnstone is the one character in the play for whom we never feel any sympathy. Although he is a corporal, he has little of Mitchem's skill in handling people and tries to exercise authority by pulling rank and by brute force. Also, unlike Mitchem, his attitude to the Japanese soldier is not governed by the cold, necessary logic of war but by a violent hatred of his enemy. Johnstone is continuously cruel to the Japanese soldier: he tears up his photographs, refuses him water and sees no humanity in the prisoner. 'It's a bloody nip'. Indeed, we get the impression that Johnstone would actually like to kill the prisoner.

Bamforth is deeply cynical about the war and about the British army. He challenges the authority of the army at every opportunity with cheeky sarcasm. He has learned the rules of the army and uses them against his superiors with quick, witty replies: 'You threatening me, Corp?'. He constantly taunts the other men saying of Whitaker, 'This boy couldn't get the home service in the sitting-room' and to Macleish 'You chasing your second stripe already?'. Bamforth shows a stronger, more humane side to his character in his relationship with the Japanese prisoner. At first he amuses himself by mocking the prisoner and treating him almost like a performing animal. After seeing the prisoner's family photographs, Bamforth warms to him until at the end of the play it is only Bamforth who is willing to defend the prisoner and say 'He's a man'. Whether Bamforth is right or wrong to defend the prisoner and the fact that he is willing to defend the Japanese soldier with his own life shows that he is more than just 'the barrack-room lawyer ... Up to every dodge and skive that's in the book.'

The strengths and weaknesses of the other characters are

also revealed in their attitudes to the Japanese soldier. Macleish has just been promoted to lance-corporal and takes his role very seriously. When he debates with Mitchem over killing the Japanese soldier he feels he would rather give up his position than be a party to a decision to kill the man. However, he appears to accept Mitchem's reasoning that the prisoner is not worth the lives of the patrol and when Bamforth appeals for his help at the climax of the play he 'continues to stare out of the window'. Whitaker is a young, vulnerable private soldier who nervously attempts to mend the radio in the face of Bamforth's teasing. He is obviously jumpy and very inexperienced and when Mitchem hands him the sten-gun, it seems only inevitable that he will shoot the prisoner in panic.

The Japanese prisoner is interesting because he reminds us that, in war, his place and that of one of the British soldiers could so easily be reversed. He has a family at home, he sneaked away from his patrol for a cigarette and is human and ordinary like the British soldiers.

Dramatic action

The Long and the Short and the Tall is a gripping, intense play. The action takes place in one set inside a deserted hut and dramatic tension arises out of the conflict between the members of the patrol. This tension is apparent near the beginning of Act One, when Bamforth's argument with Macleish almost blows up into a fight. The tension increases when Japanese voices are heard on the radio. Excitement mounts as the reality of the situation dawns on the patrol and on the audience. The tension mounts again with the capture of the Japanese soldier at the end of Act One.

As in Act One, the tension in Act Two builds up through a series of climaxes leading up to the final clash between Bamforth and Mitchem and Whitaker's incompetent shooting of the prisoner.

The play in performance

The play was commissioned in 1958, by the Oxford Theatre Group, for eight undergraduate amateur actors to stage on the Fringe of the Edinburgh Festival. When it reached the West End in 1959 it won the *Evening Standard* Drama Award for that year with Peter O'Toole playing Bamforth.

Willis Hall used the different regional accents of his original cast to reflect the way the British Army was made up of all sorts of men, with little in common except that they have all been conscripted into the army. A critic of the time, Kenneth Tynan, wrote that 'The play lacked stars and it had a downbeat (that is, anti-war) ending, in which the patrol was decimated. These facts may explain why, despite enthusiastic notices, it ran in the West End for only three months. It will, anyway, be remembered as a portent'.[1] In fact the different accents and army slang highlight the play's stark reality and add to its intense vitality. It has enjoyed success all over the world.

Willis Hall recalls that the play has been acted all over the world in different uniforms and about different wars. He was even sent a review of the performance of the play in Japan, where the reconnaissance patrol consisted of Japanese soldiers and the captured prisoner was British. Such is the play's universal appeal although the playwright insists, 'The play was conceived and written purely as an entertainment – if it also provides a "message", then that is a bonus rather than an intention.

Maureen Blakesley

---

[1] A view of the English Stage – Kenneth Tynan, Methuen, London 1984, p.253

THE LONG AND THE SHORT AND THE TALL

They say there's a troopship just leaving Bombay,
Bound for Old Blighty shore,
Heavily-laden with time-expired men,
Bound for the land they adore.
There's many a soldier just finishing his time,
There's many a twirp signing on,
You'll get no promotion this side of the ocean,
So cheer up, my lads, bless 'em all!

Bless 'em all! Bless 'em all!
The long and the short and the tall;
Bless all the sergeants and W.O.[1]s,
Bless all the corp'rals and their blinkin' sons,
'Cos we're saying goodbye to them all,
As back to their billets they crawl,
You'll get no promotion this side of the ocean,
So cheer up, my lads, bless 'em all!

They say, if you work hard you'll get better pay,
We've heard it all before,
Clean up your buttons and polish your boots,
Scrub out the barrack-room floor.
There's many a rookie has taken it in,
Hook line and sinker an' all,
You'll get no promotion this side of the ocean,
So cheer up, my lads, bless 'em all!

Bless 'em all! *etc.*

They say that the Sergeant's a very nice chap,
Oh! What a tale to tell!
Ask him for leave on a Saturday night
He'll pay your fare home as well.
There's many a soldier has blighted his life,

Thro' writing rude words on the wall,
You'll get no promotion this side of the ocean,
So cheer up, my lads, bless 'em all!

Bless 'em all! *etc.*

They say that the Corp'ral will help you along,
Oh! What an awful crime,
Lend him your razor to clean up his chin,
He'll bring it back every time.
There's many a rookie has fell in the mud,
Thro' leaving his horse in the stall,
You'll get no promotion this side of the ocean,
So cheer up, my lads, bless 'em all!

Bless 'em all! *etc.*

Nobody knows what a twirp you've been,
so cheer up, my lads, bless 'em all!

Cast of the First London Production

The Long and the Short and the Tall was first produced at the Nottingham Playhouse on 1 September 1958; it was also presented by the Oxford Theatre Group on the 'Fringe' of the 1958 Edinburgh Festival. It was directed by Peter Dews.

The play was first produced in London on 7 January 1959 at the Royal Court Theatre, then transferred to the New Theatre on 8 April 1959. It was presented by the English Stage Company in association with Oscar Lewenstein and Wolf Mankowitz, with the following cast:

465	SERGEANT MITCHEM, R.	Robert Shaw
839	CORPORAL JOHNSTONE, E.	Edward Judd
594	L/CORPORAL MACLEISH, A. J.	Ronald Fraser
632	PRIVATE WHITAKER, S.	David Andrews
777	PRIVATE EVANS, T. E.	Alfred Lynch
877	PRIVATE BAMFORTH, C.	Peter O'Toole
611	PRIVATE SMITH, P.	Bryan Pringle
A JAPANESE SOLDIER		Kenji Takaki

The play directed by LINDSAY ANDERSON
with décor by ALAN TAGG

List of Characters

465 SERGEANT MITCHEM, R.

839 CORPORAL JOHNSTONE, E.

594 L/CORPORAL MACLEISH, A. J.

632 PRIVATE WHITAKER, S.

777 PRIVATE EVANS, T. E.

877 PRIVATE BAMFORTH, C.

611 PRIVATE SMITH, P.

A JAPANESE SOLDIER

The action of the play takes place in the Malayan jungle during the Japanese advance on Singapore, early in 1942.

THE LONG AND THE SHORT
AND THE TALL

ACT ONE

Late afternoon. The curtain rises on the wooden-walled, palm-thatched, dingy interior of a deserted store-hut in the Malayan jungle. The hut is set back a few hundred yards from a tin mine which is now deserted. There is a door in the rear wall with windows on either side looking out on to the veranda and jungle beyond. The hut has been stripped of everything of any value by the mine-workers before they fled – all that remains is a rickety table and two chairs, centre stage, and a form, right. We hear a short burst of heavy gunfire in the distance – and then silence. A pause and then we hear the chirruping of crickets and the song of a bird in the jungle. A figure appears at the left hand window, looks cautiously inside and ducks away. A moment later the door is kicked open and JOHNSTONE *stands framed in the doorway, holding a sten at his hip. When the door was kicked open the crickets and the bird ceased their song.* JOHNSTONE *glances around the room and, finding it unoccupied, makes a hand signal from the veranda.* JOHNSTONE *returns into the room and is joined a few seconds later by* MITCHEM, *who also carries a sten.*

JOHNSTONE (*shifts his hat to the back of his head and places his sten on the table*). All clear. Stinks like something's dead.

MITCHEM (*placing his sten beside* JOHNSTONE'S) It'll do. To be going on with. (*He crosses to the door and motions to the rest of the patrol.*) Come on, then! Let's have you! ... Move it! Move!

One by one the members of the patrol double into the room. With the exception of WHITAKER, *who carries the radio transmitter/receiver on his back, the men are armed with rifles.*

1

SMITH *carries* WHITAKER'S *rifle. They are tired and dishevelled.*

JOHNSTONE Move yourselves! Gillo! Lacas! Lacas!

As the last member of the patrol enters the room MITCHEM *slams the door. The men stack their rifles in a corner of the hut and sit gratefully on the table.* WHITAKER *takes off the 'set' and sets it up on the table.* BAMFORTH *shrugs off his pack, places it as a pillow on the form, and makes himself comfortable.*

JOHNSTONE How long we here for?

MITCHEM (*glances at his watch*) Half an hour or so, and then we'll push off back. Better mount a guard. Two men on stag. Fifteen minute shifts.

JOHNSTONE Right ... (*He notices* BAMFORTH *who is now fully stretched out.*) Bamforth! ... Bamforth!

BAMFORTH (*raises himself with studied unconcern*) You want me, Corp.

JOHNSTONE Get on your feet, lad!

BAMFORTH What's up?

JOHNSTONE I said 'move'! (BAMFORTH *pulls himself slowly to his feet.*) You think you're on your holidays? Get your pack on!

BAMFORTH You going to inspect us, Corp?

JOHNSTONE Don't give me any of your mouth. Get your pack on! Smartish! Next time you keep it on till you hear different.

BAMFORTH (*heaves his pack on to one shoulder*) All right! O.K. All right.

JOHNSTONE Right on!

BAMFORTH *glances across at* MITCHEM.

MITCHEM You heard what he said.

BAMFORTH (*struggles the pack on to both shoulders. He speaks under his breath.*) Nit!

There is a pause. JOHNSTONE *crosses to face* BAMFORTH.

JOHNSTONE What was that?

BAMFORTH Me. I only coughed.

MITCHEM O.K., Bamforth. Just watch it, son.

JOHNSTONE	Too true, lad. Watch it. Watch it careful. I've had my bellyfull of you this time out. You watch your step. Put one foot wrong. Just one. I'll have you in the nick so fast your feet won't touch the ground. Just you move out of line, that's all.
BAMFORTH	You threatening me, Corp?
JOHNSTONE	I'm warning you!
BAMFORTH	I got witnesses!
JOHNSTONE	You'll have six months. The lot. I'll see to that, Bamforth. I'll have your guts. One foot wrong, as sure as God I'll have your guts.
BAMFORTH	Try. Try it on for size.
MITCHEM	(*crosses to intervene*) Right. Pack it in. That's both of you. (BAMFORTH *turns away from* JOHNSTONE.) I want two men for guard. First stag. Two volunteers ... Come on, come on!
SMITH	(*pulls himself to his feet*) First or second – what's the odds ...
MACLEISH	(*follows suit*) It's all the same to me.
MITCHEM	Better stay inside. Don't show yourselves. Cover the front. If anything's to come it's coming from out there.
	(MACLEISH *and* SMITH *take up their rifles and move across to cover the windows.*) How's the set?
WHITAKER	(*looks up from tuning in the radio*) It's dead. Still dis. U/s. Can't get a peep. I think the battery's giving up. Conking out.
BAMFORTH	Now he tells us! Signals! Flipping signallers – I've shot 'em. Talk about the creek without a paddle.
MITCHEM	You got any suggestions, Bamforth ...
BAMFORTH	Only offering opinions.
MITCHEM	Well don't! Don't bother. If we want opinions from you we'll ask for them. From now on keep them to yourself. Now, pay attention. All of you. We're sticking here for half an hour at the most. After that we're ... heading

back for camp. (*A murmur of relief from the men.*)
Anybody any questions?

EVANS Can we have a drag, Sarge?

MITCHEM Yeh. Smoke if you want. You can get the humpy off
your backs. Get what rest you can. Your best bet is
to grab some kip. It's a long way back. Another
thing, you'd better save your grub. I make it we'll
get back before tomorrow night – but just in case
we don't, go steady on the compo packs. O.K.?
(*There is a murmur of agreement from the men.*) I
want to have a sortie round. Outside. See how
we're fixed. Check up. Fancy a trot, Johnno?

JOHNSTONE Suits me.

*The patrol remove their packs and place them on the
floor.*

MITCHEM *and* JOHNSTONE *pick up and check their stens.*

MITCHEM Keep at it on the set, Sammy son. Have another
shot at getting through.

WHITAKER (*puts on headphones*) Right, Sarge. Don't think it's
going to do much good.

MITCHEM Keep bashing. Mac!

MACLEISH (*turns from window*) Aye?

MITCHEM We're having a stroll as far as the road. You're i/c.
We won't be long. As far as we know there's
nothing in the area for miles – but if anything crops
up – I mean, if you should see anything – don't
shoot. Unless you've got to. Right?

MACLEISH Fair enough.

MITCHEM Ready, Johnno? (JOHNSTONE *nods and follows* MITCHEM
to the door.) And keep your voices down, the lot of
you.

JOHNSTONE Bamforth! That includes you!

BAMFORTH (*who has been delving into his pack*) I heard!

MITCHEM Come on.

MITCHEM *opens the doors and exits, followed by*
JOHNSTONE. *We see them move past the window and
disappear down the veranda steps.*

BAMFORTH	(*throwing down his pack in disgust*) The creep. The stupid nit!
EVANS	Johnno's got it in for you, boyo. He'll have your guts for garters yet. He's after you. Chases you round from haircut to breakfast time.
BAMFORTH	Flipping toe-rag! He wants carving up. It's time that nit got sorted out. When this lot's over – when I get back to civvy street – I only want to meet him once. In town. That's all. Just once. Will someone see me now and hear my prayers. If I could come across him once without them tapes to come it on! I'll smash his face.
EVANS	Go on, man! He's twice the size of you! You wouldn't stand a chance, tapes or no tapes.
BAMFORTH	What do you know about scrapping? That's how you want them when you're putting in the nut. Up there. Bigger than yourself. And then you wham 'em – thump across the eyes. Straight across the eyes and then the knee and finish with the boot. All over. Send for the cleaners.
EVANS	You wouldn't fight like that, Bammo?
BAMFORTH	You want to lay me odds? I'll take fives on that. What do you know about it, you ugly foreigner? Get back to Wales, you Cardiff creep. Only good for digging coal and singing hymns, your crummy lot.
EVANS	Shows how much you know, boy. You want to see some real fighting, Bammo, you go to Cardiff on a Saturday night. Round the docks. Outside the boozers. More fights in one night than you've had hot dinners.
BAMFORTH	Country stuff, son. Country stuff. You haven't got the first idea. You ever want to see a bloke carved up? Proper? So his missus thinks he's someone else? You hand that job to London boys.
SMITH	(*glancing over his shoulder from the window*) Why don't you jack it in?
BAMFORTH	What's that?
SMITH	You heard. I said, 'give it a rest'.

BAMFORTH   I never heard your name and number in this conversation.

SMITH   I'm just telling you, that's all. I've had about enough. Bloody southerners shouting the odds. Always shouting the odds. You're like the rest. One look at a barmaid and you're on the floor.

EVANS   That's what barmaids are for, Smudge.

BAMFORTH   Good old Taff! and I always thought you were a presbyterian.

EVANS   Strict Chapel. Every Sunday.

BAMFORTH   Sunday's his day off. When he leaves the milkmaid alone. Tuesdays and Wednesdays he's going steady with a Eistedfodd.

SMITH   Come again?

BAMFORTH   One of them bints in a long black hat and bits of lace. Always singing songs. Every time you go to the pictures you see them on the news. Singing songs and playing harps and that. Hymns. Like being in church only it's outside. Dodgy move – so they can whip them up the mountainside for half an hour afterwards. Very crafty boys, these Taffs. You've got to hand it to them.

EVANS   Go on, man!

BAMFORTH   Straight up. It's straight up, son. Got any fags, have you, Taff?

EVANS   I thought you must be after something.
EVANS *takes a packet of cigarettes from his trouser pocket and offers one to* BAMFORTH *as he crosses towards him.* BAMFORTH *takes the cigarette.*

BAMFORTH   So what? As long as it's only your fags I'm after, you've no need to worry, have you, son? My name's not Johnno.

MACLEISH   (*turning at window*) Bamforth, why don't you pack it in! We've heard about enough from you.

BAMFORTH   Silence in court! Acting Unpaid Lance Corporal Macleish is just about to pull his rank! Don't it make

you sick! Doesn't it make you want to spew, eh?
Sew a bit of tape on their arms and all at once they
talk like someone else. What's the matter, Mac? You
chasing your second stripe already?

MACLEISH Are you looking for trouble, Bamforth? Because if
you are you can have it, and no messing.

BAMFORTH Ah, shut up, you Scotch haggis! Dry up, boy! It's not
your fault. All Corps are bastards, we all know that.

MACLEISH Watch your mouth! As far as I'm concerned the
tape's not worth it. Just remember that. As far as I'm
concerned I'll jack the tape tomorrow to drop you
one on. And that's a promise, Bamforth.

BAMFORTH Go stuff your tape.

EVANS *lights his cigarette behind dialogue.*

MACLEISH So just watch your mouth.

BAMFORTH Aw, come off it, son. Where I come from it's just a
name.

MACLEISH It so happens I don't like it.

SMITH Drop it, Mac. He didn't mean no harm.

MACLEISH I'm willing to accept his apology.

BAMFORTH So what's the argument about? Here, Taffy, give us a
touch, boy.

EVANS (*hands cigarette to* BAMFORTH *who lights his own and
passes it back*) I don't see, Mac, what you got to
complain about. Bammo's only having you on.
Before you got that tape you moaned about Johnno
just as much as the rest of us. More, perhaps.

SMITH Just let it drop, Taff, eh?

MACLEISH It just so happens that I accepted the rank of Lance
Corporal. Having accepted the rank, and the
responsibility that goes with it, I feel it's my duty to
back up my fellow N.C.O.s. And that decision is
regardless of any personal prejudices I might hold.

BAMFORTH King's Regulations, Chapter Three, Verse

Seventeen. The congregation will rise and sing the
hymn that's hanging up behind the door of the bog.

MACLEISH   You're just a head case, Bamforth. You're a nutter.
Round the bend.

BAMFORTH   (*jumping up on chair*) With the inspired help of our
dear friend and member, Fanny Whitaker, who will
accompany the choir on her famous five-valve organ.
All together, please! The chorus girl's lament! (*Sings.*)

My husband's a corporal, a corporal, a corporal,
A very fine corporal is he!
All day he knocks men about, knocks men about,
knocks men about,
At night he comes home and knocks me!
EVANS *joins* BAMFORTH *in the chorus.*
Singing Hey-jig-a-jig, cook a little pig, follow the band.
Follow the band all the way!
Singing Hey-jig-a-jig, cook a little pig, follow the band.
Follow the band all the way!

WHITAKER   (*glances up from tuning set*) Pack it in, Bamforth.

BAMFORTH   (*unheeding and improvising*) Order if you please.

Second verse. (*Sings.*)

Oh, as soon as this lot's through, I'll be off to
Waterloo,
And I'll be out on the town right away,
And you might as well clear off
'Cause things get bloody tough
When Bammo's on the town every day.
EVANS *joins* BAMFORTH *again in the chorus.*
Singing Hey-jig-a-jig, cook a little pig, follow the band.
Follow the band all the way!
Singing Hey-jig-a-jig ...

WHITAKER   (*rising, angrily*) Will you pack it in!

BAMFORTH   (*jumps to floor*) Hello! Our little blue-eyed signaller
doing his nut now. That's all we wanted – him!

WHITAKER   (*putting headphones on the table*) Why don't you keep
quiet, Bamforth man! I got something on the set!

BAMFORTH	'Course you did, my old flower of the East. What was it, Sammy Son? Henry Hall? Tune it up a bit – let's all have a listen. Bit of music always makes a change.
WHITAKER	I told you – I got something coming through.
MACLEISH	You think it was the camp?
BAMFORTH	We're fifteen miles from base. He's not Marconi. This boy couldn't get the home service in the sitting-room.
WHITAKER	I don't know what it was. I got something.
BAMFORTH	Fifteen miles from base! A doolally battery and ten-thumbed Whitaker i/c! What you want? A screaming miracle?
SMITH	Try them again, Sammy. Have another go.
MACLEISH	Try it on transmit.
EVANS	Tell them I'm coming home tomorrow night, boyo. Ask them in the cookhouse what's for supper. What's tomorrow? Friday? It's fish and chips!
SMITH	Do you think of anything except your stomach?
BAMFORTH	He's a walking belly.

WHITAKER *sits down and replaces headphones. He picks up the microphone and adjusts the set.* BAMFORTH *and* EVANS *approach table.*

WHITAKER	Blue Patrol ... Blue Patrol calling Red Leader ...Blue Patrol calling Red Leader ... Are you receiving me? ... Are you receiving me? ... Blue Patrol calling Red Leader ... Are you receiving me? ... Are you receiving me? Over. (WHITAKER *flicks switch to 'receive'. There is a pause during which we hear some interference – but nothing else.* WHITAKER *flicks back to 'transmit'.*) Blue Patrol calling Red Leader ... Are you receiving me? ... Are you receiving me? ... Over. (WHITAKER *again flicks to 'receive'. More interference.* WHITAKER *turns down the set and removes the headphones.*) It's dis. I think the battery's gone again.
BAMFORTH	So what's the use.
WHITAKER	I got something through, I tell you!
BAMFORTH	That's your story, boy. You stick to it.

EVANS Perhaps you imagined it, Sammy boy.

WHITAKER I had something coming through!

BAMFORTH Don't give us that. Got through! You couldn't get through a hot dinner, my old son.

MACLEISH Why don't you wrap up, Bamforth.

BAMFORTH Eight-double-seven Private Bamforth to you, Corporal Macleish. You want to come the regimental, boy, we'll have it proper.

SMITH That will be the day, Bamforth. When you can work it regimental. The biggest shower since the flood, that's you. Fred Karno's not in it. When you start giving us the heels together I'll be commanding the Camel Corps.

BAMFORTH Get your bucket and spade, Smudger, and I'll lay it on. This boy can work it any way at all. If I go creeping after tapes I'll get them.

EVANS Corporal Bamforth. N.C.O. i/c latrines. It's you who'll want the bucket, Bammo.

BAMFORTH That's all you know, you Welsh rabbit. You'd be the first to suffer. I'll have you running round the depot like a blue-house fly. Report to my tent at 1600 hours. Extra duties. Gas cape and running shoes.

EVANS And can I have a week-end pass?

BAMFORTH You what! What do you think you're on? Your father's yacht?

SMITH You get some kip, Taff. Dream of home. It's the nearest you'll get to Welsh Wales.
BAMFORTH *crosses to form, picks up his pack, punches it into a pillow and lies down.* WHITAKER, *who has been attempting to tune set, puts on headphones and switches to 'transmit'.*

WHITAKER Blue Patrol calling Red Leader .... Blue Patrol calling Red Leader .... Are you receiving me ... Are you receiving me ... Come in Red Leader ... Over.
WHITAKER *switches to 'receive' and again attempts to tune in set.* EVANS *opens his pack and takes out a crumpled magazine.* BAMFORTH *glances across at* EVANS.

BAMFORTH	What you got there, Taff?
EVANS	A book.
BAMFORTH	Two's up.
EVANS	I'll let you have it when I've finished.
BAMFORTH	(*sitting up*) What is it? Sling it across.
EVANS	(*crosses and sits on form*) My mother saves me them. (*He hands the magazine to* BAMFORTH.)
BAMFORTH	And you've been carting this around for days!
EVANS	Why not?
BAMFORTH	Here, Smudge! Seen this?
SMITH	What's that?
BAMFORTH	Taff's library.
SMITH	Yeh?
BAMFORTH	'Ladies' Companion and Home'.
SMITH	Get on!
EVANS	My mother sends it to me every week. I'm following the serial. What's wrong with that?
BAMFORTH	And you've been humping this since we left camp? Well, flipping stroll on! That's all. Stroll on.
EVANS	Why not? I've told you. I'm following the serial.
SMITH	Any good, Taff?
EVANS	Yes. It's all right. It's interesting. There's this bloke, see. In the army. Second Looey. He's knocking about with this girl who's a sort of nurse in a Military Hospital. Only before they have time to get to know each other proper, he gets posted overseas.
MACLEISH	Very exciting.
BAMFORTH	I'm crying my eyes out!
SMITH	So what happens then, Taff?
EVANS	Thing is, see, she doesn't know anything about it.
BAMFORTH	He should have taught her.
EVANS	I mean about this overseas posting. He's supposed to meet this bint one night round the back of the Nurses' Quarters.
BAMFORTH	The dirty old man!

EVANS	Who's telling this story, Bammo? Me or you?
SMITH	Get on with it, Taff.
EVANS	I'm just coming to the interesting bit if you'll give me a chance.
BAMFORTH	Come on then. Give. Let's have it. I can hardly wait to hear how Roger gets on.
EVANS	That's just it. He doesn't.
BAMFORTH	I knew there'd be a catch in it.
EVANS	He never turns up, see. Been posted. Special Mission. Got to blow up an airfield in North Africa.
SMITH	What? On his tod?
EVANS	Last one I had he'd been captured by a tribe of marauding bedouins. Savage heathens.
SMITH	Get away!
EVANS	And it finished up the last time with them tying him, hand and foot, and hanging him upside down above a blazing fire. In a sort of oasis. There was him, toasting away if you like, with the sweat dripping down off the end of his nose. And these white-robed bedouins is dancing round, waving carbines, singing heathen songs and not a care in the world. That was how it finished up in the last instalment.
SMITH	So what happens this week?
EVANS	That's just it. I can't make head or tail of it. This week starts off with him and this here nursing bint having an honeymoon in Brighton. Posh hotel, made up to captain, fourteen days' leave, smashing girl and the weather's glorious. Doesn't make sense to me. I think perhaps the old lady slipped up and sent me the wrong one first.
BAMFORTH	She slipped up all right. When she had you. Marauding bedouins! You'll lap up any old muck.
SMITH	After you with it, anyway, Taff.
BAMFORTH	You wait your turn. I'm two's up. (*He flicks through the pages of the magazine.*) Here – this is the bit I like. 'Margaret Denning Replies.' All these bints writing up 'cause someone's left them in the lurch.

SMITH   Read us one out, Bammo.

BAMFORTH   Here's a right one. Get this. 'Dear Margaret Denning. I have been walking out for six months with a corporal in the Army who's a very nice boy.' Well, there's a lie for a kick-off.

EVANS   What's she want to know?

BAMFORTH   'I like him very much and we plan to marry when the war is over. Lately, however, he has been making certain suggestions which I know are wrong.'

EVANS   Certain suggestions!

BAMFORTH   'He says I ought to agree if I love him. What shall I do? Ought I to fall in with his wishes or should I stand by my principles and risk losing him? I have always wanted a white wedding. Yours, Gwynneth Rees, Aberystwyth.' It's another Taffy!

SMITH   So what's she tell her?

BAMFORTH   'Dear Miss Taffy, I am sorry to hear that you have had the misfortune to fall in love with a corporal. The next time he starts making improper suggestions you should belt him one and marry a private.'

EVANS   It doesn't say that, does it?

BAMFORTH   (*rises and slings the magazine at* EVANS) What do you think, you ignorant burk?

EVANS   Oh, I don't know ... What do you reckon she ought to do, Smudge?

SMITH   Same as Bammo says.

EVANS   I don't know, really. I suppose you've got to wait until you're married, proper. I mean, it spoils it otherwise, they say. But if this bloke she's going out with is in the army, perhaps he's up for an overseas posting himself. I mean, things is different when there is a war. You never know, do you? He might get pushed off overseas for years, perhaps. Then where would he be?

BAMFORTH   Same as you. Up the creek without a paddle.

EVANS   That's what I'm getting at.

BAMFORTH   Wrap up, boy! Look. Don't be a creamer all your life. Have a day off. You've got a bint yourself, have you? Back home?

EVANS   I've got a girl friend. Well, of course I have. You know as well as I do. You've seen her picture.

BAMFORTH   So when you see her last?

EVANS   Embarkation leave, of course. Over a year ago. Eighteen months about.

BAMFORTH   Eighteen months! Stroll on! For all you know she could be weaning one by now. You know what Blighty is these days, do you? It's a carve up, son. A rotten carve up. Overrun with home postings wallahs, sitting back easy, sorting out the judies from Land's End to how's your father. They've got it all laid on, son. We're the mugs in this game. It's a den of vice, is Blighty. Unoriginal sin. Poles and Yanks and cartloads of glorious allies all colours of the rainbow. Even the nippers look like liquorice allsorts. They're lapping it up, Taff. You think the bints are sitting knitting?

EVANS   Mine's all right, boy. Don't you worry about that.

BAMFORTH   You mean you hope she is. You're a bloody optimist. She's probably up the mountains right this minute with a great big Yank.

EVANS   Go on, man! She's not like that.

BAMFORTH   They're all like that. So why should yours be any different?

EVANS   Well, if anything was wrong I'd hear about it.

BAMFORTH   Famous last words. What gives you that idea?

EVANS   Her mother's my auntie.

BAMFORTH   You can't marry her then! It's disgusting!

EVANS   Not my real auntie. She lives next door but one to us at home. I only call her my auntie. They've been friends, see, her mother and my mother for ever such a long time. My father's brother married her cousin, that's all. I've called her my auntie since I was a little lad.

BAMFORTH	You make it sound like rabbits.
EVANS	All the same, if anything was wrong with her, my mother would write and let me know.
BAMFORTH	You hope.
EVANS	Well, of course she would!
BAMFORTH	Look, son. Do yourself a favour, eh? Don't give me all that bull. There's only one way to keep them faithful. And that's like Smudger. Marry them sharpish and leave them with a couple of snappers running round the drum. Keep them occupied. With three or four nippers howling out for grub they don't have time to think. Right, Smudge?
SMITH	That's about it.
MACLEISH	I fail to see, Bamforth, what experience you've had on the subject.
BAMFORTH	Get lost, you Scotch haggis.
EVANS	How many you got, Smudge?
SMITH	Two.
EVANS	Boys?
SMITH	One of each.
EVANS	Boy and a girl. Must be smashing.
SMITH	What? Kids?
EVANS	Not only that. You know. Having a home, like. You know, something to go back to – afterwards. Home of your own, I mean. Wife and family and home and that. Got a house of your own yet, have you?
SMITH	Bit of a one. Council. Up on the new estate.
EVANS	Go on!
SMITH	It's all right. Bit of a garden, not much, but it's all right. Better than nothing.
EVANS	Did you do any gardening, Smudge, before you came in the army?
SMITH	Not a lot. Few veg round the back – cabbages and that, brussels, couple of rows of peas, one or two blooms. Not a lot. You know – the usual.

EVANS   I know what you mean.

SMITH   Always left the front. Made a sort of a bit of a lawn of it. Sit out on Sundays on it after dinner. Me and the Missis. Saturday afternoons sometimes – when there was football on the wireless. Just big enough to sit on – two of you. Nice bit of grass. At least, it was. I suppose the kids have racked it up.

EVANS   You don't know. Perhaps the missis has been looking after it.

SMITH   Perhaps.

EVANS   Must be worse for you, I suppose. Being stuck out here. Not like the rest of us. Having a family to think about, I mean.

BAMFORTH   Well, don't let that get you down, Taff. By the time you get out of this lot your Cardiff bint'll be miles away with her Yank.

SMITH   That'd give the neighbours something to think about, Taff.

EVANS   I'd give her something to think about if she did.

BAMFORTH   Don't be like that, Taffy. Allies is allies, my old son. No good having allies if you're not willing to share what little bit you've got.

EVANS   They wouldn't be no allies of mine, then.

BAMFORTH   You're not democratic, that's your trouble.

EVANS   (*rises and throws magazine at* BAMFORTH) I'll be after you, Bammo, if you don't give it a rest!

BAMFORTH   You and who else?

EVANS   (*crossing and playfully sparring up to* BAMFORTH) Just me, boy. You're just my size.

BAMFORTH   Come on then, you Welsh Taff! Stick me one on!

EVANS   All right! You asked for it!

EVANS *closes in on* BAMFORTH *and throws a punch.* BAMFORTH *grabs* EVANS'S *hand and twists it up and round his back.* BAMFORTH *flings* EVANS *to the floor, grabs a foot and twists it from the ankle.*

EVANS Go steady, man! You'll break my leg!

BAMFORTH You're an ignorant Welsh Taff! What are you? An ignorant Welsh Taff!

EVANS Get off my leg, you rotten fool!

BAMFORTH Say you're an ignorant Welsh Taff! Say you're an ignorant Welsh Taff!

EVANS You'll break my leg!

WHITAKER (*adjusting radio controls*) Something coming through again!

BAMFORTH (*to* EVANS) Tell them! Come on, tell them what you are!

EVANS Will you let go, man!

BAMFORTH Tell them what you are.

EVANS I'm an ignorant Welsh Taff ...I'm an ignorant Welsh Taff!

MACLEISH Bamforth! Evans! Knock it off, the pair of you!

BAMFORTH (*disengaging himself from* EVANS) So what's the matter now?

EVANS (*climbs to his feet*) You want to go easy, Bammo boy. You damn near crippled me.

BAMFORTH *and* EVANS *move across to where* WHITAKER *is seated. The radio operator is again attempting to contact base.*

WHITAKER (*flicking transmitter switch*) Blue Patrol ... Blue Patrol calling Red Leader ... Are you receiving me?... Are you receiving me? ... Over ... (WHITAKER *flicks to 'receive' and adjusts controls. He fades up the volume and we hear the crackle of interference on the set. For a moment there is also the sound of distorted speech on the radio – though the distortion and interference are too strong to make the voice distinguishable.*) It's there again!

EVANS He's right, Bammo! I heard it myself.

BAMFORTH Ah, so what.

EVANS I heard voices, Bammo!

BAMFORTH   So what does that make you? Joan of Arc? What if
            you did? Could have been from any of the mobs up
            the jungle.

EVANS   Could have been base, boyo.

            WHITAKER *takes off the headphones.*

MACLEISH   Could you make out what it was, Whitaker?

WHITAKER   (*shakes his head*) Too much interference. (*He switches
            the set off.*) I'd better leave it. No sense in wasting the
            battery. I'll leave it now till Mitch gets back.

BAMFORTH   (*crosses to form, picks up his pack and takes out a
            food pack*) You do that, son. You tell old mother
            Mitchem all about it. What a good boy you've been.
            Please, Sergeant, I've been working ever so hard.
            Please, Sergeant, I've been fiddling about with my
            little wireless all the time that you were out. Please,
            Sergeant, can I have a stripe? You make me sick.
            (*He tears open the food pack.*) Stroll on! Look here.
            Bungy. Bloody cheese again. I'll swing for that
            ration corporal one of these days.

EVANS   What do you reckon it was, Smudge?

SMITH   What's that?

EVANS   On the set. You think it might have been camp?

SMITH   Don't ask me. Whitaker's the boy to ask.

WHITAKER   Must have been. It's only fifteen miles to base. The
            nearest mob to us are nearly thirty miles up country.

EVANS   What the hell are we supposed to be doing anyway?
            Stuck here in the middle?

SMITH   Playing at soldiers. What they call a routine patrol,
            Taff. Keeping out of mischief. Out of the N.A.A.F.I.
            bar. It keeps you under control. Keeps the Colonel
            happy. It's good for morale.

EVANS   It's no good for my rotten feet. These boots, I think.
            The rubber soles that draw them.

BAMFORTH   It's a crumb patrol. It's just about the crummiest
            detail in the Far East is this, and no messing. Two
            days humping kit and two days back. Routine Patrol!

You can stick this for a game of soldiers. Talk about the P.B.I. If ever there was an all-time crumb patrol, we're on it. (*He glances round at* WHITAKER, *who has taken a needle, ball of wool and a pair of socks from his pack and is busily engaged in darning.*) What the hell are you supposed to be doing? (WHITAKER, *bent over his task, does not look up.*) You!

WHITAKER (*looks up*) What's up?

BAMFORTH What are you on like?

WHITAKER My socks.

BAMFORTH What for?

WHITAKER Kit inspection Saturday morning.

BAMFORTH Well, that just about beats the lot, does that! Now I've seen everything. Rotten stroll on! The third day's hump we're on – three days and bright boy's sweating on a kit inspection! What with him and his 'Ladies Companion' and you and your knitting! You'll still be at it when the Japs get here.

MACLEISH And where will you be, Bamforth?

BAMFORTH Me?

MACLEISH When the Japs arrive?

BAMFORTH Not here, that's certain. I wasn't meant to be a hero.

MACLEISH I gathered that.

BAMFORTH I'll tell you where I'll be, boy. Scarpering. Using my loaf. On the trot. I've got it all worked out. The lot. Tin of Cherry Blossom Dark Tan from head to foot. Couple of banana leaves round my old whatsits. Straight through Kew Gardens outside and head for the water. Like one of the locals.

EVANS You reckon you could make it, Bammo?

BAMFORTH What! If the yellow hordes were waving bayonets at me I'd be off like a whippet. You'll not see my tail for dust. There's more wog rowing boats up the coast than enough. Nip off in one of them and straight to sea.

SMITH On your own?

BAMFORTH   Tod or nothing. When the times comes, Smudge, it's going to be every man for himself.

EVANS   Go on, man. Where could you make for?

BAMFORTH   What's it matter? Anywhere but here. Desert Island. One that's loaded with bags of native bints wearing grass frocks. Settle down and turn native. Anything's better than ending up with Tojo's boys.

EVANS   You'd never do it.

BAMFORTH   That's all you know. Come down the beach and wave me off. If you've got time to wave with all them little Nippos on your trail. I'll be in the boat, Jack. Lying back and getting sunburnt with a basket of coconuts. (*'Cod' American.*) And so we say farewell to this lush, green and prosperous country of Malaya. As the sun sets in the west our tiny boat bobs peacefully towards the horizon. We take one last glimpse at the beautiful tropical coastline and can see, in the distance, our old comrade in arms and hopeless radio operator, Private Whitaker, making peace with the invading army of the Rising Sun – and the invading army of the Rising Sun is carving pieces out of Private Whitaker.

WHITAKER   (*rising*) Pack it in, Bamforth.

BAMFORTH   What's the matter, Whitto? Getting windy?

WHITAKER   Just pack it in, that's all.

BAMFORTH   Get knotted.

MACLEISH   I haven't seen anybody handing medals to you yet, Bamforth.

BAMFORTH   No, my old haggis basher. And you're not likely to. I've told you – I don't go a bundle on this death or glory stuff.

MACLEISH   So why not keep your trap shut?

BAMFORTH   Democracy, Mac. Free Speech. Votes for women and eight-double-seven Private Bamforth for Prime Minister.

SMITH   Show us your Red Flag, Bammo.

BAMFORTH   It's what we're fighting for. Loose living and six
           months' holiday a year. The General told me that
           himself. 'Bamforth,' he says to me, taking me round
           the back of the lav at Catterick. 'Bammo, my old son,
           the British Army's in a desperate position. The yellow
           peril's about to descend upon us, the gatling's
           jammed, the Colonel's dead and the cook corporal's
           stuffed the regimental mascot in the oven. On top of
           all that, and as if we hadn't got enough to worry
           about, we've got two thousand Jocks up the jungle
           suffering from screaming ab-dabs and going mad for
           women, beer and haggis. We're posting you out
           there, Bammo,' he says, 'to relieve the situation.' So
           before I had time to relieve myself, here I was.

MACLEISH   And what have you got against the Jocks?

BAMFORTH   Stroll on! He's off again! It's a joke, you thick-
           skulled nit!

MACLEISH   And I'll not stand for any of your subordinations.

BAMFORTH   Come on, boy! Come it on! Pull the tape on me
           again. That's all I want. I'll blanco your belt for you
           for twopence.

MACLEISH   When you're on duty, Bamforth, you'll take orders
           like the rest.

BAMFORTH   Get the ink dry in your pay-book first. You've not
           had the tape a month.

MACLEISH   If I'm in charge here, that's all that matters, as far as
           you're concerned. It makes no difference to you if
           I've had the tape five minutes or five years. You'll
           jump to it, boy, when I'm calling out the time.
           You'll just do as you're told, or you're for the high
           jump. (BAMFORTH *swears under his breath and turns
           away.*) Bamforth! Bamforth, I'm talking to you!

BAMFORTH   (*swings round*) Private Bamforth! I've got a rank
           myself, acting unpaid Lance Corporal Macleish!

MACLEISH   Evans!

   EVANS   Corp?

MACLEISH   Come here. (*As* EVANS *crosses towards the window* MACLEISH *tosses him the rifle.*) Here. You're on guard. Take over from me.

EVANS   Corp.

MACLEISH   (*crosses down to face* BAMFORTH) I'm not giving you any second warnings, Bamforth. When you speak to me you'll watch your mouth. I mean that, Bamforth, just watch out – or as sure as I'm standing here, I'll have you.

BAMFORTH   Try taking off your tape and saying that, you Scotch get.

MACLEISH   I've already told you, this has got nothing to do with the tape. I'm not warning you for C.O.'s orders, boy. I'm not interested in having you on the C.O.'s veranda with your cap and belt off. One word to me and I'll put your teeth down your throat. I mean that.

BAMFORTH   What with?

MACLEISH   (*raising his fists*) These. Just these.

BAMFORTH   (*unfastening his jacket*) if you want to play it the hard way, Jock ...

MACLEISH   I want to play it any way that suits me. And right now it suits me to sort you out.

SMITH   (*crossing from window*) Wrap it up, Jock.

MACLEISH   You keep out of this, Smudge. This has got nothing to do with you – it's personal between Bamforth and myself – it's got nothing to do with you.

SMITH   Like hell it hasn't. You're like a couple of kids.

MACLEISH   I said, keep out of it!

SMITH   Grow up! For God's sake grow up, the pair of you! What do you think you're on?

BAMFORTH   I'm waiting for you, Jock.

SMITH   So go on, Mac. You take a poke at him and where's it get you? You lose your tape, you're in the nick.

MACLEISH   The tape means nothing to me.

SMITH   So all right! You get six months in the nick.

BAMFORTH What are you waiting for? You're pretty big with the mouth, Jock; let's see you follow it up.

MACLEISH (*raising his fists and moving in on* BAMFORTH) You asked for it ...

SMITH (*restraining* MACLEISH) You dim Scotch crone! It's what he wants! He's dying for you to put him one on. Use your loaf! Sling in your tape and stick him one on then – if it's going to make you feel any better. Do it then. You put a finger on him now he'll come King's Regs on you so fast your feet won't touch the ground.

MACLEISH (*shrugging* SMITH *away*) I'll sort him so he never comes King's Regs again. On me or anybody else!
EVANS has turned away from the window and all interest is centred on MACLEISH *and* BAMFORTH *as the door opens and* MITCHEM *and* JOHNSTONE *enter.*

MITCHEM So what's all this in aid of?

JOHNSTONE Do your jacket up, Bamforth!

BAMFORTH Must have come undone.

JOHNSTONE And get your heels together when you speak to me, lad!

BAMFORTH (*coming slowly to attention*) Corporal.
There is an apprehensive pause as MITCHEM *crosses slowly into the centre of the room.*

MITCHEM On your feet! (WHITAKER *rises.*) Get fell in, the lot of you! Move yourselves! (*The members of the patrol, with the exception of Johnstone, fall in in single rank.*) Ted, stand by the door.

JOHNSTONE (*half closes the door and stands on guard*) Check.

MITCHEM (*he walks slowly along the line of men and turns, flicking open an unbuttoned breast pocket on* EVANS'S *jacket as he walks back.* EVANS *steps one pace out of the ranks, fastens the button and moves back in line.* MITCHEM *looks along the line of men. There is a long pause before he speaks.*) Shower! Useless shower! That's all you are. The lot of you. I could have been a regiment of ruddy Nips and I walked through that door. I walked straight in! ... Squad – shun! Stand at ease. Squad – shun! Stand at ease. Corporal Macleish!

MACLEISH   (*steps one pace forward smartly*) Sarnt!

MITCHEM   I left you in charge.

MACLEISH   Sarnt!

MITCHEM   So what happened?

MACLEISH   I ... I had occasion to reprimand ... I'm sorry, Sergeant. I forgot myself for the moment.

MITCHEM   (*pause*) So you're sorry. You forgot yourself. I leave you in charge of the section for ten minutes and the whole organization goes to pot. Ten minutes, Corporal, and you're running a monkey house! (*Pause.* MITCHEM *walks along the line and back.*) You had occasion to reprimand who?

MACLEISH   I ... I forget now, Sergeant. It was one of the men.

MITCHEM   I didn't think it was a chimpanzee. Who was it?

MACLEISH   It was something that happened in the heat of the moment. I forget now.

MITCHEM   Then you'd better remember. Smartish. Corporal Macleish. Who was the man?

MACLEISH   If it's all the same to you, Sergeant, I'd prefer not to say.

MITCHEM   For your information, Macleish, it's not the same to me. Just what do you think this is? Just what? All girls together and no telling tales? You think I'm running a Sunday School outing? 'Please, Miss, it was Jimmie Smith who sat on the tomato sandwiches but I promised not to tell.' (EVANS *laughs.*) Shut up!

MACLEISH   It was a personal matter I'd prefer to handle in my own way.

MITCHEM   Then let me put you straight, Corporal. Right now. Before it's too late. You haven't got no personal matters. Not while you're out with me. While you were settling it in your own way – sorting out your personal matters – you could have had seven men, including yourself, with their tripes on the floor. Remember that. Seven. Including me. And as far as

I'm concerned, what happens to me's important. (*Addressing the patrol.*) To look at some of you the army's not gained all that much by his incompetence. But, all the same, I brought you out and I intend to take you back. The lot of you. I'll not stand any more from any one of you who makes it awkward for the rest. I want the man who started all this argument to stand out now ... Come on, come on! (*There is a pause.*) All right. Fair enough. Have it how you want. You'll all be on fatigues when we get back to camp.

MACLEISH You can't punish all the section.

MITCHEM I can do just what I like, Corporal. I can have your guts for garters if I want.

MACLEISH It's against all army regulations.

BAMFORTH *takes one pace forward.*

MITCHEM (*crossing to face* BAMFORTH) Hello! What's this? I was wrong. It was a chimpanzee. As if I hadn't guessed. Private Bamforth, eight-double-seven.

BAMFORTH Sarnt!

MITCHEM Coming it on again. Coming it on. It's about time you and me had a few words.

BAMFORTH Sarnt?

MITCHEM Now get this, Bamforth. Get it straight. Get it in your head. Since you've been posted out to join this mob it's crossed my mind, a time or two, that you don't like the army.

BAMFORTH Sarnt.

MITCHEM It's a mutual feeling, Bamforth. The army's not in love with you. If I had you in my lot in Blighty, lad, you wouldn't last a week. I've met your kind before. I've seen men who would make a breakfast out of muck like you go in the nick and do their time and come back so that butter wouldn't melt between their crutch. Don't try and come the hard-case stuff with me, son. It doesn't work. I'm up to all them tricks myself. O.K.

BAMFORTH   Sarnt.

MITCHEM   I've watched you, lad. I've had my eye on you. Ever
since you first turned up. I've seen you try and come
it on with every junior N.C.O. that's been made up.
The barrack-room lawyer. The hard case. You can
quote King's Regs from now until the middle of next
week. Up to every dodge and skive that's in the
book. There's just one thing. It doesn't work with
me, 'cause I don't work according to the book. You
don't know anything, Bamforth. You don't know
anything at all. But if you want to try and come it on
with me I'll tell you, here and now, that I can be a
bastard. I can be the biggest bastard of them all. And
just remember this: I've got three stripes' start on you.
You're a non-runner, son, I start favourite halfway
down the course before the off. You haven't got a
chance. So now just go ahead and play it how you
want. I'm easy. (*Pause.*) Now get back into line the
pair of you. Move! (MACLEISH *and* BAMFORTH *step back
into the rank.* MITCHEM *crosses to speak to* BAMFORTH.)
And if you take my tip you'll stay in line. (MITCHEM
steps back to address the patrol.) Stand at ease! ... Easy
... (*The men relax.*) Now, pay attention – all of you.
We've had a sortie round, Corporal Johnstone and
myself; I'll try and put you in the picture now
before we set off back. The main track is about sixty
yards from here through the trees. The way we
came – and that's the way we're going back. Round
the back of here the undergrowth's so thick it
would take a month of Sundays to hack half a mile.
There's only one way out and that's where we came
in. It's over fifteen miles from here to camp and
we're moving off in fifteen minutes' time. We march
at five-yard intervals – I don't want any of you
closing up. Corporal Johnstone's breaking trail and
I'll bring up the rear. There'll be no talking. I've said
there'll be a five-yard interval between each man.
You'll keep it that way. What goes for closing up
goes twice as much for dropping back – I don't

want any of you falling out. I've told you once it's
fifteen miles, or thereabouts, to base. Due south. The
other way – north – and twenty miles as near as we
can estimate, the line's been built to keep the Nips at
bay. All positions have been consolidated. Which
means that all the mobs from round these parts have
moved up to the front – or most of them – a few
have been withdrawn. There's not a living soul, apart
from local wogs, if any, for miles from here. If any
one of you gets lost he's on his own. I don't advise it.
So you keep it five yards – dead. Anybody any
questions?

MACLEISH   Sergeant?

MITCHEM   Yeh?

MACLEISH   Have you any idea which of the mobs have moved
up country?

MITCHEM   Only what I heard when we left camp. And they
were rumours in the mess. Just about the lot, they
reckon. The Fusiliers, two regiments of Jocks and
some Artillery. You studying Military History?

MACLEISH   No. I've got ... It's my brother. He's with the
Highland boys.

MITCHEM   I see.

MACLEISH   He's my young brother. We've applied to get his
transfer to our mob. It's not come through yet.
You've heard they've moved them up already?

MITCHEM   It was just a rumour in the mess ... Anybody else
got any ticks? (*There is a negative murmur from the
men.*) That makes a change. Right then. Fifteen
minutes and we push off back. Who did first stag?

MACLEISH   Smith and myself, Sergeant.

MITCHEM   You two had better have a break. Bamforth, Evans!

BAMFORTH
EVANS   } Sarge?

MITCHEM   You're both on guard. All right. The rest of you fall
out.

BAMFORTH *and* EVANS *pick up their rifles and cross to windows.* MACLEISH *and* SMITH *cross to form and sit down.* JOHNSTONE *closes door and crosses into room as the two reliefs reach the windows.*

MITCHEM   Whitaker!

WHITAKER   Sergeant?

MITCHEM   Any joy on the set?

WHITAKER   I got something through about five minutes ago, Sarge. I don't know what it was, though. Too faint to pick it up.

JOHNSTONE   (*crossing to join* MITCHEM *and* WHITAKER) You got through to base, did you say, Whitaker?

WHITAKER   No, Corp. I got something through, though. I was telling the Sergeant. I picked up something but I don't know what it was.

JOHNSTONE   How much a week do they pay you for this, lad?

MITCHEM   It's not his fault. The battery's dis. O.K., Sammy. Have another go. Better give it one more try.

WHITAKER   (*sitting down at set*) Right, Sergeant. (*He tunes in the set behind following dialogue.*)

JOHNSTONE   What you reckon, Mitch?

MITCHEM   What's that?

JOHNSTONE   What he got.

MITCHEM   Dunno ... Suppose it must have been the camp. No one else in this area pushing out signals. With a wonky set he couldn't pick up any of the front-line mobs from here. They're out of range. So it figures that it must have been the camp.

JOHNSTONE   I'd like to put the boot in on the burk who dished us out with a u/s batt. S.O.B., that's all they are, the H.Q. men.

MITCHEM   We'll sort that out when we get back.

JOHNSTONE   I'd like to ram his pig-muck battery down his throat, that's all. Who was on duty in the battery shop?

MITCHEM   It's no good flapping over that. We'll let him have
            another go and if nothing comes up we'll pack it in.
            Push off back. We've got a negative report. It
            doesn't make a lot of difference.

JOHNSTONE   It could have been something else. It could have
            been important.

MITCHEM   It isn't. So we can sort it out when we get back.

            JOHNSTONE *and* MITCHEM *turn and listen as* WHITAKER
            attempts to make contact.

WHITAKER   Blue Patrol to Red Leader ... Blue Patrol calling Red
            Leader ... Are you receiving me? ... are you receiving
            me? ... Come in, Red Leader, come in Red Leader ...
            Over.

            WHITAKER *flicks to 'receive' and tunes in. Sound of
            interference held behind.* JOHNSTONE *and* MITCHEM
            listen for a moment and then turn away.

JOHNSTONE   Damn duff equipment! The whole damn issue's duff.

MITCHEM   (*takes out a packet of cigarettes and offers one to*
            JOHNSTONE) Fag?

JOHNSTONE   (*taking the cigarette*) Ta. (*He takes a box of matches
            from his box, strikes one, offers a light to* MITCHEM,
            then lights his own.)

MITCHEM   (*inhales deeply then exhales*) Thanks.

JOHNSTONE   Time do you reckon we'll get back?

MITCHEM   Tomorrow? 'Bout 1800 hours if we keep it up. Roll
            on. Roll on, let's get some kip.

JOHNSTONE   If you get the chance. Kit inspection Saturday
            morning. What's the betting we end up on the
            square after all? C.O.'s parade.

MITCHEM   Not this boy. I'm going to grab a week-end off, and
            chuff the expense.

WHITAKER   (*pushes the headphones on to the back of his head
            and turns in his chair*) Sarge!

MITCHEM   (*turns*) Yeh?

WHITAKER   Coming through again!

MITCHEM and JOHNSTONE *cross to the table and listen intently to the set.* WHITAKER *replaces headphones and tunes in.* MACLEISH *and* SMITH, *who have been talking together on the form, sit up and listen. There is an air of expectancy amongst the patrol. As* WHITAKER *fiddles with the controls the interference increases and dies away. A faint murmur of speech can be heard from the set.*

WHITAKER   There it is!

MITCHEM   Come on, lad! Let's be having it.

EVANS   Ask the C.O. if he loves me as much as always, Whitto boy!

BAMFORTH   Nobody loves you, you horrible Taff!

JOHNSTONE   Shut up! Pack the talking in!

WHITAKER   I've got it now!

The radio bursts into life. The voice of a Japanese radio operator comes through the set clearly. WHITAKER *turns and looks in bewilderment at* MITCHEM. *These two are the first to realize the implications. There is a slight pause, stemming from surprise, then the patrol reacts with forced humour.*

BAMFORTH   You've got it, Whitto son, all right. You've got the ruddy Japs.

EVANS   If that's the camp they're having rice for tea and my name's Tojo.

BAMFORTH   Bring on the geisha girls!

MACLEISH   A right ruddy radio operator you've turned out to be, Whitaker. You don't know whose side you're on.

MITCHEM   (*leans across and switches off the set*) Pack the talking in, the lot of you! Right, Whitaker. (WHITAKER, *who is staring in horror at the set, makes no reply.*) Whitaker, I'm talking to you, lad! (WHITAKER *looks up for the first time.*)

How strong's the battery? ... Come on, come on!

WHITAKER   It's almost gone. The battery's nearly dead.

MITCHEM   So what's your range at present? ... Whitaker, your range?

WHITAKER   (*pulling himself together slightly*) It must be under
            fifteen miles. I can't get through to camp. It could
            be ten. It might be less.
            With the exception of EVANS *the patrol begins to
            comprehend.*

EVANS   Go on, Whitto boy! You're up the creek all over.
            The Japs are past Jalim Besar. It's twenty miles away
            at least.

SMITH   We're all up the creek.

BAMFORTH   Stroll on!

JOHNSTONE   Evans! Bamforth! You're supposed to be on guard!
            Get on your posts!
            EVANS *and* BAMFORTH, *who have turned away from
            the windows during the above dialogue, return to
            their positions.*

WHITAKER   It was as clear as a bell! They could be sitting right
            on top of us!

MACLEISH   Under fifteen miles away! So what's happened to
            the lads up country?

MITCHEM   Shut up.

MACLEISH   What's happened to the forward boys?

MITCHEM   Shut up.

MACLEISH   I've got my brother posted up out there!

MITCHEM   Shut up! Johnno, check the stens.

JOHNSTONE   (*crossing to table where he checks* MITCHEM'S *sten and
            his own*) Right.

MITCHEM   (*crossing to* MACLEISH) Now just shut up. Listen. All of
            you. Evans, Bamforth, don't turn round. I want your
            eyes out there. You got that, both of you? (BAMFORTH
            and EVANS *nod.*) Then ram a round apiece up your
            spouts. (BAMFORTH *and* EVANS *release the safety
            catches on their rifles, withdraw the bolts and slam
            them home.*) O.K. Now put your safety catches on.
            (BAMFORTH *and* EVANS *hesitate a moment and then
            comply.*) O.K. That's fine. That's all we need. No
            more than that. (*He crosses centre stage to address
            the patrol.*) Fred Karno's mob. That's what you are.
            Fred Karno's mob. There's half of you been

shooting off your mouths for days on end on how you'd fix the Japs. To listen to you talk you'd win the ruddy war on bread and jam. You've heard one slimy Nippo on the set and now you're having second thoughts. You make me laugh, that's what you do to me – make me want to laugh. (JOHNSTONE *has now finished his examination of the stens.*) O.K., Johnno?

JOHNSTONE   Both O.K.

MITCHEM   (*to the patrol*) You've heard one Nippo on the set. That might mean anything at all. It might mean that they've broken through, up country, and are pouring down. If that's a fact, then chuff your luck. That's all – just chuff your luck. They might be swarming out there now – like ants. And if they are and I'm with crumbs like you, I'm up the creek myself and that's a fact. (*The patrol murmurs uneasily.*) But all you know so far is that you've heard a Nippo griping on the set. And that could mean that somewhere in this festering heat one lousy bunch of Japs have wriggled in behind our lines – that could be half a dozen me. It could be less than that. It could be half a dozen joskins like yourselves. Six or seven – five or six – or even two or three poor helpless wet-nurse ginks who somewhere, close to here, are running round in circles, doing their nuts, because they've heard young Whitto pushing out a signal back to base. If that's the way things are with them, the bloke who's calling out the time for 'em has got my sympathy. I wish him luck. He's up to the short hairs in it like myself and so I wish him luck. (*The confidence of the men has been largely restored – one or two are even amused.*) I'll tell you what we're going to do. We're moving off. Right now. (*Murmur of relief from the men.*) We're going back. It's odds on that they're just a buckshee bunch of Harries like yourselves. All the same, we're not waiting to find out. The orders for the movement back still stand. Evans, Bamforth, you'll stay on guard until the others have got their gear on and are ready to move off back.

The men begin to struggle into their webbing equipment.

JOHNSTONE Come on, then! Move yourselves! We've not got time to play about!

MITCHEM Macleish and Smith! (MACLEISH *and* SMITH *pause in assembling their kit.*) Soon as you've got into your gear, relieve the two on guard and let them get theirs on.

(MACLEISH *and* SMITH *nod and return to their task.*)
Quick as you can.

JOHNSTONE (*picks up the stens and hands one to* MITCHEM) You want me to lead off back?

MITCHEM (*nods*) Crack the whip a bit. Set a steady pace. I want to try and do it in one stint.

JOHNSTONE I'm with you.

BAMFORTH (*unnoticed by the others,* BAMFORTH *suddenly tenses himself and raises his rifle. He flicks off the safety catch and takes aim*) Sarge ... Sarge!

MITCHEM (*sensing* BAMFORTH'S *urgency*) Hold it, all of you! (*The men are still and silent.*) What's up?

BAMFORTH I thought I saw a movement down the track ... It's there again!

MITCHEM (*to the patrol*) Get down! Get out of sight! (*Apart from the two men on guard and* MITCHEM, *the members of the patrol stoop below the level of the windows.*) How many of them? Can you see?

BAMFORTH (*lowers his rifle*) No. Out of sight again. Behind the trees. Heading this way.

MITCHEM, *his head down below window level, moves across the hut to join* BAMFORTH *at the window.*
JOHNSTONE *moves across to join* EVANS.

MITCHEM Which way they coming from?

BAMFORTH (*pointing*) Along the track. Down there. 'Bout fifty yards.

MITCHEM Evans?

EVANS Can't see a ruddy thing from here, Sarge. Not as far as that.

JOHNSTONE	There's a clump of blasted bushes in the way.
MITCHEM	Were they Japs?
BAMFORTH	Might have been anything. Only had a glimpse.
MITCHEM	Are you sure, Bamforth?
BAMFORTH	Meaning what?
MITCHEM	You saw anything at all, lad?
BAMFORTH	You think I'm going round the bend!
MITCHEM	All right. We'll take your word for it. If there is anyone down there they should come into sight again just by that bit of ...
BAMFORTH	(*nudges* MITCHEM *and points again*) A Jap!
MITCHEM	I've got him. On his own. (*Turns slightly from window.*) Now keep still, all of you. This one's on his tod. Could be a scout. He hasn't spotted this place up to press. Got him, Johnno?
JOHNSTONE	Can't see anything for this ruddy bush. Where-abouts?
MITCHEM	Just less than fifty yards. Straight ahead ... Got him, have you?
JOHNSTONE	Not yet. What do you think he's on?
BAMFORTH	He's ... He's looking round for something. In the grass. Looking for something ... Bending down.
JOHNSTONE	Think he's found the trail, Mitch? Up to here?
MITCHEM	Looks like that. Found something by the way he's carrying on.
	BAMFORTH *bursts into laughter.*
MITCHEM	Shut up!
BAMFORTH	Found the trail! He's found the trail all right! He's found a place to have a crafty smoke.
EVANS	He's what, Bammo?
BAMFORTH	Having a drag. He's lighting up a fag. Well, the crafty old Nip. The skiving get. Caught red-handed. Nip down and ask him for a puff, Taff.
MITCHEM	Off all the rotten luck. He would choose this place. We'll wait and see'f he pushes off ... (BAMFORTH

slowly raises his rifle and takes careful aim. MITCHEM
*swings round and knocks the rifle out of aiming
position.*) I said no noise!

BAMFORTH   I had him right between the cheeks! I couldn't miss!
He's on his tod!

MITCHEM   What gives you that idea? Do you think they march
off by the dozen for a sly swallow?

JOHNSTONE   What's happening?

BAMFORTH   He's up. He's standing up and nicking out the nub.
He's going back. The way he came ... Stopped ...
Turning round ... He's coming back. He's found the
track up here. He's coming up.

MITCHEM   Move it then, the rest of you. Let's have you over by
the wall! And bring your gear.

MACLEISH, WHITAKER *and* SMITH *pick up their rifles and
the kit and scurry across the rear wall of the hut.*

MITCHEM   (*peering round the window*) Bamforth, Evans, down
on deck! (BAMFORTH *and* EVANS *drop below window
level.*) And stay there all of you. There's just a
chance he might not come inside. In case he does –
Johnno ... (MITCHEM *indicates the door.* JOHNSTONE
nods and sidles across to stand by the door. MITCHEM
peers round window.) If he should come in – you
grab. Without a sound. I'll cover the outside in case.
Still coming up ... Close to the wall as you can. He
might not see us yet.

WHITAKER   (*notices the radio which is still standing on the table*)
Sarge! The set!

MITCHEM   Oh God, lad! Get it! Quick! (WHITAKER *moves as if to
cross to table, but changes his mind and hugs the
wall in terror.*) Get the set! (WHITAKER *is still afraid to
move.* SMITH *is about to fetch the radio when we hear
the sound of feet on the wooden veranda.*) Too late!
*The members of the patrol squeeze up against the
wall as* MITCHEM *edges away from the window out of
sight.* JOHNSTONE *tenses himself. The* JAPANESE SOLDIER
can be heard clattering on the veranda for several

seconds before he appears at the left-hand window. He peers into the room but fails to see the patrol and is just about to turn away when he notices the radio on the table. He stares at it for a short while and then moves out of sight as he crosses along the veranda towards the door. A further short pause, JOHNSTONE *raises his hands in readiness. The door opens and the* JAPANESE SOLDIER *enters. As he steps into the room* JOHNSTONE *lunges forward and grabs the* JAPANESE, *putting an arm round his throat and his free hand over the soldier's mouth.* MITCHEM, *holding the sten at his hip, darts out of the door and covers the jungle from the veranda.* JOHNSTONE *and* THE PRISONER *struggle in the room.*

JOHNSTONE   Come on then, one of you! Get him! Quick! …
Evans! Do for him! (EVANS *crosses and raises his rifle, releasing the safety catch.*) No, you burk! You want to do for me as well? Come on, lad! Use your bayonet! In his guts! You'll have to give it hump. (EVANS *unsheaths his bayonet and approaches the struggling figures.*) Sharp then, lad! Come on! Come on! You want it in between his ribs. (EVANS *raises the bayonet to stab* THE PRISONER, *who squirms in terror.*) Not that way, lad! You'll only bust a bone. Feel for it first, then ram it in. Now, come on, quick! (EVANS *places his bayonet point on the chest of* THE PRISONER, *who has now stopped struggling and is cringeing in the grip of* JOHNSTONE.) Come on! Come on! I can't hold on to him for ever! Will you ram it in!

EVANS   (*steps back*) I … I can't do it, Corp.

JOHNSTONE   Stick it in! Don't stand there tossing up the odds! Just close your eyes and whoof it in!

EVANS   I can't! I can't! Corp, I can't!

JOHNSTONE   Macleish!

MACLEISH   Not me!

JOHNSTONE   Smith! Take the bayonet! Don't stand there gawping. Do the job!

SMITH   For God's sake do it, Taff. Put the poor bastard out of his misery.

EVANS   (*proffering the bayonet to* SMITH) You!

BAMFORTH   (*crossing and snatching the bayonet from* EVANS)
Here. Give me a hold. It's only the same as carving
up a pig. Hold him still.

BAMFORTH *raises the bayonet and is about to thrust it
into the chest of the prisoner as* MITCHEM *enters,
closing the door behind him.*

MITCHEM   Bamforth! Hold it!

BAMFORTH   (*hesitates, then moves away*) I'm only doing what
I'm told.

MITCHEM   Just hold it, that's all. I want this one alive. You'll
have your chance before we've done. You can count
on that. So pack in all this greyhound with a bunny
lark. He's not the only one; you'll have your chance.
How is he, Johnno? Is he going to do his nut?

JOHNSTONE   Scared stiff. He's going up the wall. I've had enough
of him – he stinks of garlic and wog grub. He won't
try anything – I wouldn't trust his mouth.

MITCHEM   Hold him for a sec. (MITCHEM *crosses close up to* THE
PRISONER.) You speakee English? Understand?
Compronney? Eh? Eh? You speakee English talk?
Trust me to cop a raving lunatic. You! I want no
noise, see? Understand? No noise! Quiet. (MITCHEM
points to his mouth and shakes his head.) No
speakee! Keep your trap shut, eh? Now get this,
Tojo. Understand. You make so much as a mutter
and I'll let Jack the Ripper have a go at you.
(MITCHEM *indicates* BAMFORTH, *who is still holding the
bayonet.* THE PRISONER *cringes in* JOHNSTONE'S *grip.*)
O.K.? (MITCHEM *points again to his mouth and* THE
PRISONER *nods vigorously.*) Good. One murmur, Jap,
and Laughing Boy will slit your guts up to your
ears. Universal talk. I think I'm getting through to
him at last. Bamforth!

BAMFORTH   (*crossing to* MITCHEM) Sarge?

MITCHEM   Put the carving knife away before he dies on us of
fright.

BAMFORTH   (*turns the bayonet over in his hand and makes a quick, playful gesture with the weapon towards* THE PRISONER'S *throat.* THE PRISONER *struggles again in* JOHNSTONE'S *arms*) Boo!

MITCHEM   Bamforth! Jack it in! I said put the cutlery away.

BAMFORTH   All right! (*He crosses and returns the bayonet to* EVANS *who replaces it in the sheath.* THE PRISONER *calms down.*) Thanks, Taff.

MITCHEM   Right, Johnno. He'll behave himself. He'll be a good lad. Put him down.

JOHNSTONE *pushes* THE PRISONER *away.* MITCHEM *gestures with the sten and* THE PRISONER'S *arms fly up above his head.* THE PRISONER *is a small, round, pathetic and almost comic character, armed to the teeth in a Gilbertian fashion: a revolver in a leather holster is slung round his chest and a string of hand grenades swings from his waist. A long two-edged bayonet hangs from his belt. He wears a drab, ill-fitting uniform, peaked cap and a white silk muffler is tied round his throat. As* THE PRISONER *stands alone and afraid in the centre of the hut the patrol cluster round to examine him.*

EVANS   He looks as if he's going to fight the war himself.

MACLEISH   He's not exactly what you'd call a handsome bloke.

MITCHEM   All right, get back. What do you want, Jock? A blonde? I'll fix it so it's Rita Hayworth walks in next. Move it! Back!

The members of the patrol cross over to the left as MITCHEM *ushers* THE PRISONER *towards the right-hand wall.*

JOHNSTONE   Come on then! Move yourselves! He doesn't put the wind up you lot now? You're round him like a lot of lambs that's had their first taste of milk. Two minutes since you wouldn't touch him with a barge pole. None of you!

MITCHEM   Bamforth! Take the armoury away.

BAMFORTH   (*crosses to* THE PRISONER, *who cringes away as he* *approaches*) Stand still, you nig! Unless you want the boot!

(BAMFORTH *proceeds to remove the weapons from* THE PRISONER, *also checking him for any further arms.*)

JOHNSTONE	A right lot I've got landed with! Not one of you had the guts to give me a hand.
MACLEISH	You weren't in need of help. You cannot order men to put a bayonet in an unarmed prisoner.
JOHNSTONE	What do you think they dish you out with bayonets for? Just opening tins of soup?
MACLEISH	They're not to put in prisoners of war!
JOHNSTONE	You know what you can do with yours. You wouldn't know which end is which!
MACLEISH	If the need should arise I'll use a bayonet with the next. But I've no intention of using one on any man who can't defend himself.
JOHNSTONE	You burk!
MACLEISH	He was a prisoner of war!
JOHNSTONE	Prisoner my crutch!
MACLEISH	There's such a thing as the Geneva Convention!
JOHNSTONE	He's carting more cannon than the Woolwich Arsenal! If he'd have pulled the pin on one of them grenades we'd all of us been up the shoot! You think that he'd of us second thoughts before he put the mockers on the lot of us?
BAMFORTH	(*places* THE PRISONER'S *arms on the table*) That's about the lot.
MITCHEM	Which of you men's supposed to be on guard? The war's not won because you've copped a Nip!
EVANS	I was, Sarge.
MITCHEM	Get on your post and stay there, lad. Who else?
BAMFORTH	Me.
MITCHEM	I've got another job for you. Anybody else that's not done stag so far?
WHITAKER	I haven't been on guard yet, Sarge. I was on the set.
MITCHEM	Then get on now. Take Bamforth's number.

(EVANS *and* WHITAKER *pick up their rifles and cross to the windows.*) Bamforth!

BAMFORTH Sarge?

MITCHEM (*offering his sten to* BAMFORTH) Here. Cop on for this. You're looking after Tojo here. I think he fancies you. If he tries to come it on he gets it through the head. No messing. He's on your charge. Look after him.

BAMFORTH (*shakes his head, refusing the sten*) Like he was my only chick. (BAMFORTH *picks up* THE PRISONER'S *bayonet from the table.*) I'll settle for this. (*He crosses towards* THE PRISONER.) Down, Shortarse. (*He motions* THE PRISONER *to sit on the form.*) Put your hands up on your head. (THE PRISONER *looks at* BAMFORTH *in bewilderment.*) I said, get your hands up on your head! Like this! See! Flingers on the blonce! All light? (BAMFORTH *demonstrates and* THE PRISONER *complies.* BAMFORTH *is delighted.*) Hey, Taff! See that, did you? He did it like I said! Flingers up on blonce. I only talk the lingo natural!

EVANS (*turning at window*) I always knew you were an Oriental creep at heart, man!

BAMFORTH You've not seen nothing, yet – get this. (*To* THE PRISONER.) Allee lightee. Flingers up to touch the loof. Come on, come on! Touch the loof, you Asiatic glet! (BAMFORTH *raises the bayonet and* THE PRISONER *cringes away.*) He's a rotten ignoramus.

MITCHEM All right, that'll do. Pack it in. Now listen, all of you. We're taking this boy back to camp with us. I want to get him there in one piece.

JOHNSTONE It's a bit dodgy, isn't it, Mitch?

MITCHEM Happen.

JOHNSTONE It's going to be a dodgy number as it is. You don't know how many more of them there are out there.

MITCHEM Not yet.

JOHNSTONE They could be coming down in strength.

MITCHEM They might.

JOHNSTONE	And if they are we're up the creek all right. We've got enough on getting this lot back. They've no experience. We'll have to belt it like the clappers out of hell. We can't afford to hang about.
MITCHEM	We'll shift.
JOHNSTONE	But if we've got to cart a prisoner along as well ...
MITCHEM	He'll go the pace. I'll see to that.
JOHNSTONE	You're in charge.
MITCHEM	That's right. Corporal Macleish! Smith!
MACLEISH	Sergeant?
SMITH	Sarge?
MITCHEM	I've got a job for you two. Outside. (MACLEISH *and* SMITH *exchange glances.*) I want the pair of you to nip down as far as the main track. Look for any signs of any more of them. O.K.?
MACLEISH	You want us to go down now, Sarge?
MITCHEM	Straight away. If the coast's clear we want to belt off back. Smartish.
MACLEISH	Right.
MITCHEM	Take it steady – careful – but don't make a meal out of it. The sooner we can make a start from here the better.
	MACLEISH *and* SMITH *strap on their ammunition pouches.*
MACLEISH	Supposing we should ... make contact?
MITCHEM	Don't. Not if you can help it. If you see anything that moves – turn back. Mac, you'd better take a sten. Take mine. (MACLEISH *crosses and takes sten and a couple of clips of ammunition from* MITCHEM. SMITH *unsheaths his bayonet and clips it on his rifle.*) Come on. (MITCHEM, MACLEISH *and* SMITH *cross to the door.*) What's it like out, Evans?
EVANS	Quiet. Quiet as a grave.
WHITAKER	Nothing this side, Sarge.
MITCHEM	Cover them as far as you can down the track.
	(EVANS *and* WHITAKER *nod.* MITCHEM *opens the door*

slowly and ushers SMITH *and* MACLEISH *on to the veranda*.) Off you go.

EVANS   So long, Smudger, Jock.

MITCHEM   (*closes door and crosses to where* BAMFORTH *is guarding* THE PRISONER) How's he behaving himself?

BAMFORTH   (*fingering the bayonet*) All right. He hasn't got much choice.

MITCHEM   (*to* THE PRISONER) You listen to me. Understand? You come with us. We take you back. We take you back with us. Oh, blimey ... Look ... Bamforth.

BAMFORTH   Yeh?

MITCHEM   Tell him he can drop his hands. He isn't going to run away.

BAMFORTH   Hey, Tojo! Flingers off blonce. Flingers off blonce! (THE PRISONER *raises his hands in the air*.) Not that, you nit! Here, that's not bad though, is it? He's coming on. He knows his flingers already. Good old Tojo! (THE PRISONER *smiles*.) Now let them dlop. Dlop, see! Down! (BAMFORTH *demonstrates and* THE PRISONER *slowly drops his hands*.) He picks up quick. He's a glutton for knowledge.

MITCHEM   (*speaks slowly and carefully*) You – come – with – us! Back! We – take – you – back! (THE PRISONER *is mystified*.) Back to camp! (MITCHEM *turns away*.) What's the use ... (MITCHEM *crosses to table*.)

BAMFORTH   I'll work on him. I'll chat him up a bit.

JOHNSTONE We should have done him first time off.

MITCHEM   I'm giving the orders!

BAMFORTH   Flingers on blonce. (THE PRISONER *complies happily*.) Dlop flingers. (*Again* THE PRISONER *obeys*.) Get that! He dlops them like a two-year-old!

JOHNSTONE Just keep him quiet, Bamforth, that's all. We don't want any of the funny patter!

BAMFORTH   I'm teaching him to talk!

JOHNSTONE Well don't! Mitch, we've got fifteen miles to slog it back. We've got no set. We know the Japs are

coming through – so someone's waiting for a report
– and quick. We can't drag him along – suppose he
tries to come it on? One shout from him with any of
his boys around we're in the cart. The lot of us.

MITCHEM   So what do you suggest?

JOHNSTONE Get rid of him. Right now. You going soft?

MITCHEM   And if we do? You want to make out the report
when we get back?

JOHNSTONE Report! You want to make out a report! Because we
do a Jap? We whip him out and knock him off, that's
all. We can't take prisoners. We're out to do a job.

MITCHEM   Reports on him don't bother me. And if I've got to
do for him – I will. I'll knock him off myself. You
think I'm stuffing my nut worrying about a Jap? One
Jap? I've got six men. They're my responsibility. But
more than that, and like you say, I've got a job to
do. So all right. So I'll do it. Now you tell me what's
going on out there? (MITCHEM *indicates the window.*)
Just tell me how many Nips have broken through
and where they are right now. You want to wait
and count them for yourself?

JOHNSTONE I want to slog it back!

MITCHEM   All right. That's what we're going to do. With him.
(*Points to* THE PRISONER.) With Tojo there. Because if
anybody knows the strength of Nips behind our
lines it's him. So far on this outing it's been the
biggest muck-up in the history of the British Army,
and that's saying a lot. We've wandered round, the
set's packed in, we've no idea what's going on and
if there ever was an organized shambles – my God,
this is it. Now things have changed. We've copped
on to a lad who's going to make this detail worth its
while. If I can get him back to camp what they'll get
out of him could do more good than if you should
serve a score and one. So he's important for what
he knows. And I'll leave any man on this patrol
behind – including you – before I'll say goodbye to

	him. Going soft? Do you think I give a twopenny damn about his life? It's what he knows.
JOHNSTONE	Suppose he comes the ab-dabs on the way?
MITCHEM	He won't.
JOHNSTONE	But if he does? He only needs to start playing it up at the wrong time. He only wants to start coming it on when we're close to his muckers.
MITCHEM	I've said he won't.
JOHNSTONE	What if he does?

MITCHEM *and* JOHNSTONE *glance across at* THE PRISONER.

MITCHEM	I'll put the bayonet in his guts myself. (*Pause.*) You'd better check these Jap grenades. Might come in handy.

MITCHEM *and* JOHNSTONE *turn to table to check the grenades.* THE PRISONER'S *hand goes up to his breast pocket.* BAMFORTH *raises the bayonet threateningly.*

BAMFORTH	Watch it, Tojo boy! Just watch your step! I'll have it in as soon as look at you!
MITCHEM	(*glancing round*) What's up with him?
BAMFORTH	Going for his pocket.

THE PRISONER *gestures towards his pocket.*

MITCHEM	All right. See what he wants.
BAMFORTH	(*still threatening with the bayonet, he opens* THE PRISONER'S *breast pocket and takes out a cheap leather wallet*) It's his wallet.
JOHNSTONE	Sling it out the window.
MITCHEM	Let him have it. Check it first.

BAMFORTH *briefly inspects the interior of the wallet.*

JOHNSTONE	You're going to let him have it!
MITCHEM	It costs us nothing. No point in getting him niggly before we start.
BAMFORTH	Looks all right, Sarge.
MITCHEM	Give it him.

BAMFORTH *hands the wallet to* THE PRISONER, *who opens it, extracts a couple of photographs and hands one to* BAMFORTH.

BAMFORTH	It's a photo! It's a picture of a Nippo bint! (THE

PRISONER *points proudly to himself.*) Who's this, then, eh? You got wife? Your missis? (THE PRISONER *points again to himself.*) It's his old woman! Very good. Japanese girl very good, eh? Good old Tojo! She's a bit short in the pins, that's all. But very nice. THE PRISONER *passes another photograph to* BAMFORTH.) Here! Get this! Nippo snappers, Sarge. Two Jap kids. Couple of chicos. You got two chicos, eh? (THE PRISONER *does not understand.* BAMFORTH *points to photograph and holds up two fingers.*) Two! See? You got two kids. (THE PRISONER *shakes his head and holds up three fingers.*) Three? No, you stupid raving imbecile! Two! (BAMFORTH *points again to the photograph.*) One and one's two! Dinky-doo-number-two! (THE PRISONER *holds up his hands to indicate a baby.*) What another? Another one as well! Well, you crafty old devil! You're as bad as Smudge. (BAMFORTH *returns the photographs to* THE PRISONER, *who replaces them carefully in his wallet and returns it to his pocket.*) Let's see if you still know your lessons. Flingers up on blonce! (THE PRISONER *complies.*) Dlop flingers! (*Again* THE PRISONER *is happy to obey.*) Stroll on! See that! He got it right both times! He's almost human this one is!

MITCHEM   All right, Bamforth, jack it in!

JOHNSTONE   We should have done him when he first turned up.

MITCHEM   (*crossing to* EVANS) Where have them two got to?

EVANS   No sign yet, Sarge.

MITCHEM *peers out of window.* BAMFORTH takes out a *packet of cigarettes and puts one in his mouth. He replaces the packet in his pocket and feels for a box of matches as his glance falls on* THE PRISONER, *who is looking up at him.* BAMFORTH *hesitates, then transfers the cigarette from his own mouth to* THE PRISONER'S. *He takes out another cigarette for himself.* JOHNSTONE *rises and crosses to* BAMFORTH. BAMFORTH *is still looking for a match as* JOHNSTONE *takes out a box, strikes one and offers* BAMFORTH *a light.*

BAMFORTH	Ta. (JOHNSTONE *holds out the match for* THE PRISONER. *As* THE PRISONER *leans across to get a light,* JOHNSTONE *knocks the cigarette from his mouth with the back of his hand.*) What's that in aid of?
JOHNSTONE	He gets permission first!
BAMFORTH	I gave him it!
JOHNSTONE	Since when have you been calling out the time!
BAMFORTH	I don't ask you before I give a bloke a fag!
JOHNSTONE	This one you do!
BAMFORTH	Who says?
JOHNSTONE	I do, lad! (*Making a sudden grab for* THE PRISONER *and attempting to tear open his breast pocket.*) I'll fix his photos for the Herb as well!
MITCHEM	(*turns*) Corporal Johnstone!
BAMFORTH	(*drops the bayonet and clutches* JOHNSTONE *by his jacket lapels. He brings his knee up in* JOHNSTONE'S *groin and, as* JOHNSTONE *doubles forward,* BAMFORTH *cracks his forehead across the bridge of* JOHNSTONE'S *nose*) Have that!
MITCHEM	(*crossing towards the fight*) Bamforth!
	BAMFORTH, *unheeding, strikes* JOHNSTONE *in the stomach and pushes him to the floor.*
JOHNSTONE	(*pulling himself to his feet*) All right. You've done it this time, Bamforth! You've shot your load. As sure as God you'll get three years for that.
BAMFORTH	(*picks up bayonet*) You try and make it stick.
MITCHEM	You're on a charge, Bamforth. You're under open arrest.
BAMFORTH	He started it!
MITCHEM	Tell that to the C.O.
EVANS	(*raising his rifle*) Sarge! There's someone coming up the track!
MITCHEM	(*crosses to window*) Whereabouts?
EVANS	Just coming through the trees.
	JOHNSTONE *picks up his sten and crosses to join* WHITAKER.

MITCHEM   It's all right. It's Macleish and Smith. Cover them up
          the track.

JOHNSTONE   (*aiming the sten*) I've got them.

EVANS   Looks as if they're in a hurry over something.
        A pause before we hear MACLEISH *and* SMITH *clatter up
        on to the veranda.* MITCHEM *opens the door and they
        enter the room. They lean against the wall
        exhausted.*

MITCHEM   Anybody after you? (MACLEISH *shakes his head.*)
          What's up then?

EVANS   What's the hurry, Smudger boy? You look as if
        you've had the whole of the Japanese army on your
        tail.

SMITH   (*out of breath*) We have ... Near enough.

MITCHEM   Sit down a tick. (SMITH *and* MACLEISH *cross to the table
          and sit down.* MITCHEM *crosses to join them.*) Now,
          come on – give. Let's be having it.

MACLEISH   (*regaining his breath*) They've broken through. In
           strength. There's hundreds of them moving down
           the main trail back.

MITCHEM   Go on.

SMITH   They must have come through our defence lines
        like a dose of salts. They're pouring down. Happy
        as a lot of sand boys. Not a mark on any one of
        them. Up front the whole damn shoot's collapsed.

MITCHEM   You weren't spotted?

MACLEISH   (*shakes his head*) They're not even looking for
           anybody. They seem to know they've got this area
           to themselves. Smudge and myself got down in the
           long grass. They've got no scouts out. Nothing. Just
           strolling down the trail as if they owned the jungle...

MITCHEM   Do you think they'll find this place?

MACLEISH   Not yet a while. We watched about a company
           march past. There was a break then in the file. We
           managed to cover up the entrance of the trail up
           here.

SMITH   We stuffed it up with bits of branch and stuff.

MITCHEM   Good.

MACLEISH	The next batch came along as we were finishing. We patched up what we could and scooted back.
JOHNSTONE	So what happens now?
MITCHEM	It's put the kybosh on the journey back. We can't move out of here just yet, and that's a certainty.
MACLEISH	You never saw so many Japs. There must be at least a thousand of them now between ourselves and base. We're right behind their forward lines.
MITCHEM	(*crosses downstage and turns*) Let's say, for now, they march without a stop. That brings them close up on the camp before tomorrow night. If they've got stuff up in the air to back them up – and if they don't know back at base they've broken through – the base mob gets wiped up.
MACLEISH	But they'll know by now the Japs are through.
MITCHEM	We can't count on that.
JOHNSTONE	If the main road's free, they'll have heavy transport loads of Nips chugging down before tomorrow.
MITCHEM	Let's hope the Engineers have sewn that up. They'll have it mined at least. No, this is the back way in. Cross country – and it's hard graft cutting trail – they'll have to do the lot on foot.
JOHNSTONE	So?
MITCHEM	So that means we can put the blocks on them. We get there first.
JOHNSTONE	You think the Japs are going to open ranks and let us pass?
MITCHEM	What's the time now? (*He glances at his watch.*) It'll be dark in just over an hour. We might make it then.
JOHNSTONE	And so you think we stand a chance at creeping through a regiment of ruddy Nips!
MITCHEM	What's your suggestion?
JOHNSTONE	We haven't got a chance.
MITCHEM	We've got no choice. We might make it in the dark and in that shrub. They'll be blundering about themselves. At least we know the way – we've done

it coming up. It's all new ground to them. We might creep through.

JOHNSTONE (*indicating* THE PRISONER) What? With him in tow?

MITCHEM (*glancing across at* THE PRISONER) No ... We're ditching him. Whitaker!

WHITAKER (*turning at window*) Sarge?

MITCHEM (*indicating set*) Come on. You'd better give it one more try.

WHITAKER I don't think it'll do any good, Sarge. The battery's nigh on stone dead.

MITCHEM Try it, lad! Don't argue. Relieve him, Smith.

SMITH *crosses to take* WHITAKER'S *place at the window as* WHITAKER *crosses to table and sits at set. He switches on to 'transmit' and pauses.*

MITCHEM Come on, lad! Get on with it! We haven't time to mess about.

WHITAKER (*turning in his chair to speak to* MITCHEM) If there are any Japs near here switched to receive they'll get a fix on us.

MITCHEM That can't be helped. Come on, come on!

WHITAKER (*putting on headphones and tuning in*) Blue Patrol to Red Leader ... Blue Patrol to Red Leader ... Are you receiving me? ... Are you receiving me? ... Come in Red Leader ... Come in Red Leader ... Over ... (WHITAKER *switches to 'receive' and tunes in. We hear the crackle of interference.*) Nothing yet ...

MITCHEM Come on, Sammy son, come on...

WHITAKER (*adjusting tuning dial*) There's something here ... (*The interference dies away and we hear the voice of the Japanese radio operator as before.*) It's the Jap transmitting. Same as before.

MITCHEM Get off the ruddy line, you Nip!

The voice continues in Japanese for a few seconds and then stops. It continues in taunting broken English.

OPERATOR Johnnee! ... Johnnee! ... British Johnnee! We – you –

come – to get ... We – you – come – to – get.

WHITAKER *starts up in fear and* MITCHEM *pushes him back into his chair. The patrol turn and look at* THE PRISONER. THE PRISONER, *noting that all attention is centred on himself, and feeling that he is expected to entertain the patrol, raises his hands in the air and slowly places them on his head. He smiles round blandly in search of approbation.*

THE CURTAIN FALLS

ACT TWO

Thirty minutes later. As the curtain rises we discover BAMFORTH,
EVANS *and* JOHNSTONE *asleep on the ground by the wall, left,*
MACLEISH *is guarding* THE PRISONER, *who is still sitting on the form
where we left him.* SMITH *and* WHITAKER *are standing at the rear
windows.* MITCHEM *is seated at the table cleaning his sten. A bird
sings out in the jungle and* WHITAKER *starts and raises his rifle.
He realizes the cause of his fears and glances round the room in
embarrassment. The other occupants, however, have not noticed
this lapse on the part of* WHITAKER. MITCHEM *places his sten on the
table and crosses to* SMITH.

MITCHEM	All O.K., Smudge?
SMITH	All O.K..
MITCHEM	Sammy?
WHITAKER	Nothing to report here, Sarnt. What time is it now?
MITCHEM	(*glances at his watch*) 'Bout quarter past. (*He returns to his task at the table.*)
SMITH	Why don't you buy a watch?
WHITAKER	I had one, Smudger. Bought one down the town once. When I had a week-end off one time. Twenty-eight bucks it was. A good one.
SMITH	Twenty-eight! For a watch? They saw you coming, and no mistake.
WHITAKER	No, man, it was a good one, I tell you. Smasher. Told you the date and what day it was and all that. Little red jewels for numbers and a sort of little moon came up to tell you when it's night.
SMITH	You can see when it's night. It gets dark.

51

WHITAKER Aye, but it was a smashing watch, Smudge. You can't get watches like that one was in Blighty. There was a bloke in the N.A.A.F.I. offered me forty bucks for it once. Forty bucks and a sort of Siamese ring he was wearing.

SMITH You took it?

WHITAKER I turned it down.

SMITH What for?

WHITAKER I'm not a fool altogether. You wouldn't get another watch like that. I was going to give it to the old man as a present when we get back home. I wouldn't have minded the ring, though. That was a beauty. Peruvian gold.

SMITH I thought you said it was Siamese?

WHITAKER It was. It had a kind of Siamese bint on the front. Doing a sort of dance with her knees bent in front of a temple – her hands sticking up in the air.

SMITH So where is it?

WHITAKER It wouldn't come off his finger.

SMITH I mean the watch.

WHITAKER I wasn't going to swop the watch for that, boy. I've got more sense than that. I could have flogged it for a fortune back in Blighty – if I hadn't have been going to give it to the old man for his present.

SMITH So where is it then?

WHITAKER I lost it. Well, it got knocked off. It was half-inched back in camp. I left it in the ablutions one morning while I went off to the latrine. I wasn't gone above two minutes – it was about the time they were giving us fruit salad twice a day and dehydrated spuds. When I came back it was gone. Two minutes at the most. My tooth-paste was gone as well. That was the most expensive trot to the lav that I ever had, I know that. Boy, there's some thieving rascals round the camp.

SMITH You should have reported it to the R.S.M. Had a personal kit inspection.

WHITAKER	Ah, what would have been the use? I wouldn't have got it back. If anybody pinched a watch like that he wouldn't leave it lying around in his locker, man. He'd want his head looking at. I've never bought another one since then. I haven't had the heart for it. What time did you say it was, Sarnt?
MITCHEM	I've just told you.
WHITAKER	I forgot.
MITCHEM	Quarter past.
WHITAKER	Roll on. Roll on my relief and let me get my head down. Sergeant Mitchem?
MITCHEM	What is it? What's up now?
WHITAKER	What time we setting off?
MITCHEM	I'll tell you. When it's time to move. We won't leave you behind. Don't worry. No need to flap.

WHITAKER, *who has been talking to take his mind off other things, relapses into silence.*

MITCHEM	(*takes out his water bottle and has a drink. He glances across at* THE PRISONER *and hands the water bottle to* MACLEISH) Here, Jock, see'f Noisy Harry wants a gob.
MACLEISH	Right, Sarge. (MACLEISH *offers the water bottle to* THE PRISONER, *who accepts it gratefully.* THE PRISONER *takes two pulls at the bottle, wipes the mouth, recorks it and hands it back to* MACLEISH *who, in turn, returns it to* MITCHEM.) Your bottle.
MITCHEM	(*glances up from cleaning the sten as* MACLEISH *places the water bottle on the table*) Right. Thanks.
MACLEISH	(*anxious to start a conversation*) He doesn't seem a bad sort of bloke.
MITCHEM	Who? Him?
MACLEISH	I suppose there's good and bad wherever you look. I mean, he's quiet enough.
MITCHEM	What did you expect?
MACLEISH	Oh, I don't know ... You hear these tales. I suppose it is all over? Up country, I mean?

MITCHEM   You saw them coming through, lad.

MACLEISH   Aye. Only I was wondering if they'd taken many prisoners themselves. The Japs, I mean.

MITCHEM   Search me.

MACLEISH   It seems to me ... I've been thinking it over, like, in my mind. And I was thinking, at the little time it's taken them to get down here – as far as this – they couldn't have had a lot of resistance. I mean, do you think it's possible there's been a sort of general jacking in from our lads?

MITCHEM   Happen. I don't know.

MACLEISH   I mean, if there'd been anything like a scrap at all they'd still be at it now, if you see what I mean.

MITCHEM   It follows. They might still be at it, for all we know. Mopping up. We don't know how much of the front still stands – if any. It could be just a section of the line packed in.

MACLEISH   I was wondering about Donald – that's my brother.

MITCHEM   Yeh?

MACLEISH   Well, if you work on the assumption that it's all over – that they've come straight through ...

MITCHEM   It doesn't do to count on 'ifs' in this lark.

MACLEISH   No. But if they have, it's likely that they've copped a lot of prisoners, the Japs. That stands to reason.

MITCHEM   That's fair enough.

MACLEISH   So it's possible my brother is a P.O.W. already.

MITCHEM   There's a chance of that.

MACLEISH   You hear so many stories – you know, on how the Japs treat P.O.W.s.

MITCHEM   Pretty rough, they reckon.

MACLEISH   I'm not so sure. You hear all kinds of things. As if they're almost ... animals. But this bloke seems a decent sort of bloke.

MITCHEM   It's hard to tell.

MACLEISH I mean, he's a family man himself.

MITCHEM So what? Is that supposed to make a difference?

MACLEISH He's human at least.

MITCHEM What do you want for your money? Dracula? Look, son, forget the home and family bull. You put a bloke in uniform and push him overseas and he's a different bloke to what he was before. I've watched it happen scores of times.

MACLEISH But if a bloke's got a wife and family himself ...

MITCHEM You get a bloke between your sights and stop to wonder if he's got a family, Jock, your family's not got you. There's half of them got families and most of them are nigs like us who don't know why we're here or what it's all in aid of. It's not your worry that. You're not paid to think.

MACLEISH I used to wonder ... Worried me a lot ... I've often wondered, if it came to the push, was it inside me to kill a man.

MITCHEM It's inside all of us. That's the trouble. Just needs fetching out, and some need more to bring it out than others.

MACLEISH You know – when we got this one – when he first came in – I couldn't do it. I just couldn't move. I don't know now whether I'm sorry or I'm glad.

MITCHEM You'll do it if it's necessary.

MACLEISH I'm not worried, mind. I mean, I'm not afraid or anything like that. At least, I don't think I'm afraid no more than anybody else. I think if it was outside it would be different. The way you look at things, I mean. If it was him or me. Something moving about in the trees – something you can put a bullet in and not have to ... have to look into its eyes.

MITCHEM I've told you once – you think too much. Outside or else in here – what's the difference?

MACLEISH   Outside he's got a fighting chance.

MITCHEM   Don't come that. It's not a game of darts. You can't wipe the board clean and start all over again. Mugs away. The mugs have had it. There are far too many mugs about. We're all mugs, and I'll tell you why. I'll tell you what's the trouble with this world, Jock – bints.

MACLEISH   (*amused*) Go on!

MITCHEM   It's right. Straight up. They cause more upset than enough. Half the scrapping in this world is over judies. There's half the blokes out here now who'd be sitting back in Blighty still with wangled home postings if it wasn't for a bint. It's bints who go a bundle over uniforms. You take a bloke – an ordinary bloke who gets called up. He doesn't want to go. He doesn't want to come out here, or if he does he's round the bend. Then, one day, this poor Charlie winds up with a bird – it happens to us all in the end. She whips him up the dancers once and that's the end of that. She likes the colour of his uniform and that makes him feel big. Six months before he was sitting behind a desk, copping on a weekly, picking his nose and chatting up the pigeons on the window-sill. Now – all at once – he feels like he's a man. Before he knows where he is he's standing on the boat deck and the bint's waving him off from the docks with a bitsy hanky and tears clogging up her powder. My hero stuff. The captain blows the whistle on the bridge. The gang-plank's up. There's a military band on the quay-side, best boots and battledress, playing 'Where was the Engine Driver?' 'Goodbye Dolly I must leave you.' So there stands Charlie Harry, five foot four in his socks, and feeling like he's Clive of India, Alexander the Great and Henry Five rolled into one.

MACLEISH   You're a real one for handing out the patter.

MITCHEM   Few weeks after that he's on his back with his feet in the air and a hole as big as your fist in his belly. And he's nothing.

MACLEISH (*uneasily*) I reckon that it's you who thinks too much.

MITCHEM I'm not a thinking kind of man. I look at facts. It happens to us all. Do you think that bint is going to float off to a nunnery? (*Indicating* THE PRISONER.) Just take a look at him. For all you know, his missis back in Tokyo thinks he's a sort of Rudolph Valentino.

MACLEISH If she does she wants glasses.

MITCHEM Happen so. But that's the way it is. So just you drop the home and bint and family bull. You might end up like him.

MACLEISH How's that?

MITCHEM What do you mean?

MACLEISH So how does he end up when we head back?

MITCHEM We're stacking him.

MACLEISH That's what I understood. You mean we're leaving him behind.

MITCHEM It's a sticky number as it is. We've got to go right through the lot of them. We'd never make it with a prisoner as well. It's odds against us now. With him as well we wouldn't stand a chance.

MACLEISH I was beginning to get quite fond of him.

MITCHEM He's no use now. He couldn't tell us any more than we know already. He's no cop to us. He's lost his value.

MACLEISH Are we going to leave him here?

MITCHEM Yeh.

MACLEISH In the hut?

MITCHEM That's right.

MACLEISH That's a bit risky, isn't it?

MITCHEM How do you mean?

MACLEISH Suppose they find the track up here? Suppose the Japs come up and cut him loose? He lets them know what time we left. How many there are of us.

MITCHEM He won't.

MACLEISH Aye, but if he did? If they knew how much start we had on them they'd catch us up in no time. If he could tell them that...

MITCHEM He won't.

MACLEISH There's nothing to stop him.

MITCHEM I've told you twice, he won't!

MACLEISH I mean, it seems to me the risk's as big as if we tried to take him back with us. They know we're somewhere in this area. It's only a matter of time before they find this place.

MITCHEM They don't know anything.

MACLEISH They know we're round about here somewhere. Why else would they be bashing out the patter on the set?

MITCHEM It's regular procedure with the Nips. Routine stuff. They push out muck in English on the off-chance. To put the wind up anyone who might be hanging round. It doesn't mean a thing.

MACLEISH We won't have time to cover up the entrance of the track again. We'll have to go straight through. I mean, the path up here is going to be wide open. It's going to be like putting up a sign. The minute we move out of here it's ten to one they'll find the track straight off.

MITCHEM They'll find him, that's all.

MACLEISH Aye. But he can tell them. About us.

MITCHEM He won't tell anybody. Anything.

MACLEISH What's to stop him?

MITCHEM I'll see to that.

MACLEISH I fail to see what you can do about it.

MITCHEM You don't have to.

MACLEISH You're not ... you're not going to knock him off?

MITCHEM Just do your job, Mac, that's all.

MACLEISH You're not going to knock him off!

MITCHEM Do you want to do it?

MACLEISH He's a P.O.W.!

MITCHEM Shut up.

MACLEISH	You can't kill him!
MITCHEM	That's my worry.
MACLEISH	The man's a prisoner-of-war!
MITCHEM	There's thousands more like him between this mob and base. It's him that's playing at home today, not you and me. If anybody's P.O.W.s it's us – not him.
MACLEISH	He gave himself up.
MITCHEM	He should have had more sense.
MACLEISH	You can't just walk him outside and put a bullet into him.
MITCHEM	No. I know that. It'd make too much noise.
MACLEISH	(*glancing down at the bayonet he holds in his hand*) Oh, God ... Not that.
MITCHEM	Do you think I'm looking forward to it?
MACLEISH	Not that ... Not like that.
MITCHEM	I've got six men and one report to come out of this lot. If I hang on to him it could work out I lose the whole patrol. I could lose more than that. For all we know, the unit's sitting back on its backside with thousands of these little Harries streaming down in that direction. You reckon I should lose my sleep over him?
MACLEISH	There must be something else.
MITCHEM	There isn't.
MACLEISH	There's another way.
MITCHEM	It's no good!
MACLEISH	Suppose we tied him up and ditched him in the bushes. Round the back, say. Out of sight. So it took a while for them to find him.
MITCHEM	It's no good.
MACLEISH	It's a damn sight better than doing him in.
MITCHEM	Is that what you think? Use your head. Do you think I haven't thought of that already? We hide him up out here he starves to death. That could take days. Do you think that's doing him a favour?
MACLEISH	What do you think you're doing?

MITCHEM   Me? My job. What they pay me to do.

MACLEISH   To knock of P.O.W.s!

MITCHEM   To put first things first.

MACLEISH   It's bloody murder, man!

MITCHEM   (*crossing to* MACLEISH) 'Course it is. That is my job. That's why I'm here. And you. (*He indicates his stripes.*) That's why I'm wearing these. And I'm wearing these 'cause I'm the one who makes the decisions. Like this. If you want to do that, Jock, you can have my job right now. Here and now. It stinks. To me, it stinks. It stinks to me to do for him. But, come to that, the whole lot stinks to me. So what am I supposed to do? Turn conshi? Jack it in? Leave the world to his lot?

MACLEISH   I've got a brother who could just be sitting back – right now. Like him.

MITCHEM   Jock, I can smell your kind a mile away.

MACLEISH   What's that supposed to mean?

MITCHEM   The Bamforth touch.

MACLEISH   Bammo?

MITCHEM   You're as bad as Bamforth, boy.

MACLEISH   Me! You think that I'm like Bamforth?

MITCHEM   All the bloody way.

MACLEISH   You're off your nut.

MITCHEM   It's the book. According to the book. You can't forget the book. All along the road – the book. It doesn't work. You'd make a right pair. Nothing to choose between you – except that Bammo fiddles it to suit himself. You like to come the greater glory of mankind.

MACLEISH   It seems to me you're talking out of the back of your head.

MITCHEM   Don't you believe it. And to think that it was me who put you up for that tape. You're right – I must be going round the bend.

MACLEISH   You can strip me when you want. You know what you can do with the tape.

MITCHEM	And wouldn't that be lovely, eh? Wouldn't that just suit you down to the ground?
MACLEISH	How's that?
MITCHEM	It lets you out of this. On the ground floor. You're back in the ranks. One of the boys and none of the responsibility.
MACLEISH	Perhaps I'd rather be one of the boys.
MITCHEM	You can say that again. So why did you cop on for the tape in the first place?
MACLEISH	I've never complained about doing my job – that doesn't mean I'm willing to be a party to what you're suggesting.
MITCHEM	Lad, have you got lots to learn. How did you reckon it was going to be? Like in the comics? Fearless Mac Macleish charging up a little hill with a score of grenades and highland war cries? Wiping out machine-guns single-handed? The gallant lance-jack gutting half a dozen Nips with a Boy Scout penknife and a Union Jack? Walking back to Jock-land with enough medals to sink a destroyer?
MACLEISH	You're talking through your hat.
MITCHEM	(*crossing to* MACLEISH) Yeh? Reckon, do you? Happen so. Perhaps you're right. You happen haven't got the guts for that. I'll tell you this much, boy – a touch like that's the easiest thing on earth. The army's full of square-head yobs who keep their brains between their legs. Blokes who do their nuts for fifteen seconds and cop a decoration, cheer boys cheer, Rule Britannia and death before dishonour. All right. Why not? Good luck to them. Lads like that win wars so they should have the medals. They deserve them. But a touch like this comes harder. The trouble is with war – a lot of it's like this – most of it. Too much. You've that to learn.
MACLEISH	There's nothing you can teach me.
MITCHEM	You're dead right there.
MACLEISH	I make my own decisions.

MITCHEM	It's the only way. I'll just say this much, Jock: before you get much older you'll grow up. If this war shapes the way I think it will, you'll grow up, lad, in next to no time. (*He crosses towards table.*) Before the month is out you'll do a dozen jobs like this before you have your breakfast. (*He sits at table.*) So just think on.
WHITAKER	(*turning at window*) Sergeant Mitchem.
MITCHEM	You again? What is it now?
WHITAKER	I ... I was wondering what the time was now.
MITCHEM	Not again! What's up? Do you want changing?
WHITAKER	It was just that I was wondering what time it was.
MITCHEM	(*glances at his watch*) Half-past – all but.
WHITAKER	I thought it must be getting on that way.
MITCHEM	Another minute and I'll give the lads a shout.
	THE PRISONER *gestures towards his breast pocket.*
MACLEISH	Sarnt ... Sergeant Mitchem!
MITCHEM	(*glancing round*) I ought to change my name. What's your complaint?
MACLEISH	It's him. I think there's something that he wants.
MITCHEM	If it's outside he can't. Tell him to hold it.
MACLEISH	Something in his pocket.
MITCHEM	Again? Oh – all right. O.K. See what it is. You get it for him.
MACLEISH	Right. (*To* THE PRISONER.) Now, you behave yourself, my lad. (MACLEISH *opens* THE PRISONER'S *breast pocket and extracts the wallet.*) Is it this? (THE PRISONER *shakes his head.* MACLEISH *replaces the wallet and takes a cigarette case from* THE PRISONER'S *pocket.*) Is this it? Is it this that you were wanting? (THE PRISONER *nods his head.*) Is it all right for the prisoner to have a drag, Sarge?
MITCHEM	Yeh. O.K.
MACLEISH	(*he hands the case to* THE PRISONER *who takes out two cigarettes, offering one to* MACLEISH) Who? Me? You're giving one to me? (*He takes the proffered cigarette.* THE PRISONER *closes the case and places it on the*

form.) That's ... that's very kind of you. (MACLEISH
takes a box of matches from his pocket.) My name's
Macleish. (*Points to himself.*) Macleish. Do you
understand? (*Pointing again to himself.*) Macleish –
me. (*He points to* THE PRISONER.) Who – are – you?
(THE PRISONER *places his hands on his head.*) Is that
the only thing you know?

MITCHEM (*crosses towards the sleeping figures of* BAMFORTH,
EVANS *and* JOHNSTONE) I shouldn't get too attached to
him. (*He shakes* JOHNSTONE.) Johnno! ... Johnno!
MACLEISH *gives* THE PRISONER *a light behind following
dialogue.*

JOHNSTONE (*wakes and sits up*) Yeh?

MITCHEM Half-past.

JOHNSTONE (*rubs his eyes*) Right.

MITCHEM (*crosses and shakes* BAMFORTH) Come on, come on!
Wakey-wakey, rise and shine. Let's have you!
(BAMFORTH *sits up as* MITCHEM *crosses to wake* EVANS.)
Evans! Evans, lad!

EVANS (*sitting up*) I feel horrible.

MITCHEM You look it. Get your skates on. Let's be having you.
The sun's burning your eyes out. Move yourselves,
then!

EVANS What's the time, Sarnt?

MITCHEM Don't you start that as well. It's turned half-past. (*He
crosses to table and sits down, then glances across at
BAMFORTH and EVANS, who have not, as yet, made any
attempt to rise.*) Come on! I said, move yourselves!

BAMFORTH I've got a mouth like the inside of a tram driver's
glove.

EVANS Had a good kip, Bammo boy?

BAMFORTH What? Kipping next to you? Kipping with a Taff?
How could I? (*He lights a cigarette.*) I was having a
smashing dream, though, son.

EVANS Who was she?

BAMFORTH Why should I tell you – you dream about your own.
You dream about the milk-maids, Taff. They're

more in your line. Have a sordid nightmare. The
bints in my dreams have got class. Society bints.

EVANS I bet they are.

BAMFORTH Straight up.

JOHNSTONE What do you know about society bints, Bamforth?

BAMFORTH All the lot. You have to kiss them first.

Evans laughs.

JOHNSTONE (*now on his feet*) Got all the answers, haven't you?

BAMFORTH Most of them. You've got to have with bints.

MITCHEM All right, less of the love life, Bamforth. Let's have
you on your feet.

BAMFORTH *and* EVANS *rise and adjust their uniforms
as* JOHNSTONE *crosses to the table.*

JOHNSTONE Anything fresh?

MITCHEM (*shakes his head*) Not yet. We haven't tried the set
again. Nothing new outside. (*He glances up as*
BAMFORTH *crosses towards the door.*) What you on,
then?

BAMFORTH (*at door*) I want to go outside!

MITCHEM What for?

BAMFORTH I can't help it.

MITCHEM I don't want anybody moving round outside.

BAMFORTH It's not my fault!

MITCHEM All right. Go on. And make it sharp.

BAMFORTH (*to* SMITH) So what am I supposed to do? Write out
an application?

MITCHEM If you're going, Bamforth, you'd better get off now.

BAMFORTH (*opens door*) All right! (*To* SMITH.) So long.

EVANS (*crossing to stand by* SMITH) Bring me back a
coconut, boy!

BAMFORTH (*as he exits*) Fetch your own.

MITCHEM Whitaker!

WHITAKER (*turning at window*) Sarge?

MITCHEM	Cover him outside.
WHITAKER	Righto.
JOHNSTONE	What time we pushing off?
MITCHEM	Another half an hour, happen. Maybe more. As soon as it gets dark enough to give us cover.
JOHNSTONE	(*inclining his head towards* THE PRISONER) And him?
MITCHEM	It's settled what we're going to do with him.
JOHNSTONE	(*takes out a packet of cigarettes and offers one to* MITCHEM) Who?
MITCHEM	(*shakes his head, declining the cigarette*) Meaning what?
JOHNSTONE	(*lights his own cigarette before answering*) Who gets to do the job?
MITCHEM	Are you volunteering?
JOHNSTONE	(*blows out a cloud of smoke*) I don't mind.
MITCHEM	Do you know, I think you would at that.
JOHNSTONE	Somebody's got to do it.
MITCHEM	It's got to be arranged yet, has that. We could draw lots. I don't know – perhaps I ought to do the job myself.
JOHNSTONE	It wants doing quick.
MITCHEM	I know.
JOHNSTONE	And quiet.
MITCHEM	I know.
JOHNSTONE	It's a skilled job.
MITCHEM	I know all that!
JOHNSTONE	So it wants somebody who knows what they're doing. You or me. We could toss up.
MITCHEM	Look – don't try and teach me my job, eh?
JOHNSTONE	Only trying to help. Just making a suggestion. It wants a professional touch. (*He glances across at* THE PRISONER *who is still smoking.*) Who gave him that?
MITCHEM	You what?
JOHNSTONE	(*crosses and grasps* THE PRISONER'S *wrist*)

Macleish! Have you been keeping him in smokes?

MITCHEM   I gave him permission.

JOHNSTONE   (*releasing* THE PRISONER's *hand in disgust*) All right. Carry on.

MACLEISH   I didn't give him the fag, in any case. (*He indicates his own cigarette.*) As a matter of fact, it was him who gave me this.

JOHNSTONE   Going mates already?

MACLEISH   'Course not.

JOHNSTONE   What's up then? Do you fancy him?

MACLEISH   I can't see that there's any harm in accepting a fag from the bloke.

JOHNSTONE   You wouldn't.

MACLEISH   There's no harm in that!

JOHNSTONE   Not much. You ought to go the whole way, lad. Turn native. You'll be eating your connor from banana leaves next. I wouldn't touch his stinking wog tobacco.

MACLEISH   It's just an ordinary cigarette.

JOHNSTONE   You what? Let's have a shufti.

MACLEISH   (*holding up the cigarette for* JOHNSTONE's *inspection*) It's just the same as any other cigarette. There's no difference.

JOHNSTONE   (*taking the cigarette from* MACLEISH) You wouldn't chuckle. It's the same all right. There's not a bit of difference. It's a Blighty fag. (*He snatches the cigarette from* THE PRISONER.) They're British smokes. They're British Army issue!

MITCHEM   (*rising and crossing to join* JOHNSTONE) Give us hold. (JOHNSTONE *hands one of the cigarettes to* MITCHEM, *who examines it closely.*) They're army issue right enough. He must have thieved them from the lads up country.

MITCHEM, MACLEISH *and* JOHNSTONE *turn and look at* THE PRISONER.

EVANS   (*crossing to join the group*) What's the matter, Jock? What's happened?

MACLEISH   It's him. It's bright boy there. He's carrying a load of British issue fags.

EVANS   How did he get hold of them?

JOHNSTONE   How do you think? You can have three guesses. The thieving Nip!

MITCHEM   (*drops the cigarette and grinds it beneath his heel*) If there's one thing gets my hump it's knocking off – it's looting.

JOHNSTONE   (*holding out the cigarette to* MACLEISH) Well, come on, Jock, you'd better finish it. You're the one he gave it to. You reckon you're his mate.

MACLEISH   (*snatching the cigarette*) I'll ram it down his rotten throat! I'll make him eat the rotten thing! (*He hesitates – for a moment we feel that he is about to carry out the threat – he hurls the cigarette across the room.*)

JOHNSTONE   You don't want to waste it, Jock. Not now you've started it. You never know how much that fag has cost. He's happen stuck his bayonet end in some poor Herb for that.

EVANS   There's some of them would kill their mothers for a drag.

MITCHEM   (*to* MACLEISH) And you were telling me how they treat P.O.W.s.

EVANS   He wants a lesson, Sarge. He ought to have a lesson taught to him.

MACLEISH   I'll kill him!

MITCHEM   Will you? You swop sides quick. (*There is a pause as they turn to look at* THE PRISONER, *who, uncertain of their attitude towards him, picks up the case, opens it and offers a cigarette to* MITCHEM.) Stick 'em! (MITCHEM *strikes the case from* THE PRISONER'S *hand.* THE PRISONER *raises his hands and places them on his head – on this occasion, however, the action is without humour.*) Thieving slob!

JOHNSTONE   (*raising a fist*) Who goes in first?

MITCHEM   Hold it.

JOHNSTONE   (*advancing threateningly on* THE PRISONER) Who gets first crack?

MITCHEM   Hold it a sec!

JOHNSTONE *checks himself.*

MACLEISH   (*almost to himself*) My brother's just nineteen. He's only been out here a couple of months. I haven't seen him since he docked. They whipped him straight up country. He's only just nineteen. (*A loud appeal to the patrol – as if in the hope of receiving a denial.*) For all I know he's dead!

MITCHEM   Jock – see if he's lugging anything else he's lifted from our lads.

MACLEISH   (*moving to* THE PRISONER) Get up! Get on your feet! (THE PRISONER *cowers on the form and* MACLEISH *jerks him savagely to his feet.*) Do as you're told! (MACLEISH *goes through* THE PRISONER'S *pocket and removes the wallet.*) There's this.

JOHNSTONE   (*taking the wallet*) I'll have a look at what's in this. You carry on.

MACLEISH   (*as* THE PRISONER *reacts slightly at the loss of the wallet*) Stand still!

MACLEISH *goes through* THE PRISONER'S *trouser pockets and removes the usual miscellaneous assortment of articles: handkerchief, keys, loose change, etc.* MACLEISH *places these on the form.* JOHNSTONE, *slowly and carefully, tears the photographs into pieces and drops these and the wallet on the floor.* THE PRISONER *starts forward and* MACLEISH *rises and strikes him across the face.* BAMFORTH, *who has just re-entered from the veranda, notices this incident.*

MACLEISH   I said, stand still!

BAMFORTH   What's up? What's he done to ask for that?

EVANS   He's been looting, Bammo. From our lads.

BAMFORTH   (*crossing to join the group around* THE PRISONER) He's been what?

MACLEISH   We caught him with a fag-case stuffed with British Army smokes.

BAMFORTH   You Scotch nit! You dim Scotch nit! I gave him
            them!

MITCHEM   You did?

BAMFORTH   I'm telling you. I gave him half a dozen snouts!

EVANS   You gave them him?

            MACLEISH *edges away from* THE PRISONER *and* BAMFORTH
            positions himself between THE PRISONER *and the*
            members of the patrol.

BAMFORTH   What's the matter, Taff? Are your ears bad? I slipped
            him half a dozen nubs!

MACLEISH   I didn't know. I thought ... I thought he'd knocked
            them off.

JOHNSTONE   (*to* BAMFORTH) And who gave you permission?

BAMFORTH   I've had this out with you before. You show where
            it says I have to grease up to an N.C.O. before I
            hand out fags. What's mine's my own. I decide what
            I do with it.

MACLEISH   How was I to know? I ... I've told you, boy, I
            thought he'd knocked them off.

BAMFORTH   You know what thought did.

MACLEISH   (*searching for words*) How was I to know? ... mean,
            he gave one of them to me ... I'd lit it up ... I was
            having a drag ... I was half-way down the lousy
            thing before I realized, you know – I mean, before I
            knew it was a Blighty fag ... So how was I to feel? ...
            What would you have done? ... You tell me, Bammo
            .... I could have choked, you know ... I've got a
            brother who's up country.

BAMFORTH   If he's dropped in with a gang of Nips who think
            like you, God help the kiddie. God help him!

MACLEISH   I thought he'd looted them!

BAMFORTH   And so you pull the big brave hero bull. The raving
            highlander. Aren't you the boy? So what you waiting
            for? Well, come on, Jock, finish off the job!
            (BAMFORTH *grabs* THE PRISONER, *pinning his arms, and*
            swings him round, holding him towards MACLEISH.)

Come on, come on! Come on, he's waiting for the hump. Let's see you slot him, Jock! Drop him one on! Let's see you do your stuff! Smash his face for him! Drop him one on!

MACLEISH   Lay off it, Bamforth.

MITCHEM   O.K., Bamforth, jack it in.

BAMFORTH   Haven't any of you got the guts to go the bundle? You were snapping at the leash when I walked in. What about you, Taff? You want to have a crack at him?

MITCHEM   I said, drop it.

BAMFORTH   (*loosing his hold on* THE PRISONER) I didn't start it.

THE PRISONER *sits on form and returns the articles to his trouser pockets.*

EVANS   It was a mistake, Bammo.

BAMFORTH   You bet it was.

EVANS   We thought he'd whipped them.

BAMFORTH   (*stoops and picks up the wallet and a piece of the torn photographs*) You bastards. You even had to rip his pictures up. You couldn't leave him them even!

EVANS   I'll give you a hand to pick them up.

BAMFORTH   You couldn't even leave him them!

EVANS   (*bends down and collects the torn pieces of the photographs*) Happen he can stick them together again, Bammo. Here's a bit with a head on it. He could stick them together, easy enough, with a pot of paste and a brush.

BAMFORTH   Aw ... Dry up, you Welsh burk.

EVANS   (*rises and crosses to* THE PRISONER) Tojo ... Tojo, boy. (THE PRISONER *looks up.*) I got your pieces for you. You can stick them together again. Pot of paste and a bit of fiddling and they'll be right as rain. (MITCHEM *and* MACLEISH *move away from* THE PRISONER.) Good as ever they was ... Well, not quite as good, happen, but if you don't mind the joins and do them careful it won't matter, will it? (EVANS *holds out the torn pieces, but* THE PRISONER, *fearing further blows, is hesitant in accepting them.*) Go on, Tojo son, you have them back. Better than nothing, anyway. (THE PRISONER *takes the torn fragments and examines them one by one.*) Some of them are only torn in two. All the face is there on that one. (THE PRISONER *continues to examine the pieces.* EVANS *stoops to retrieve a scrap of a photograph which he had overlooked previously.*) A bit here I missed. Looks like a little bit of a little bit of a girlie. (*He examines the fragment closely.*) Oh no, it's a boy, is that. (*He presses the scrap into the hands of* THE PRISONER.) You'll ... you'll be needing that as well.

BAMFORTH   (*handing the wallet to* EVANS) Here, Taff, stick him this.

EVANS   Right, boyo. (*He hands the wallet to* THE PRISONER.) And here's your wallet, Tojo boy.

MACLEISH   (*picks up the cigarette case from the floor and gives it to* BAMFORTH) He'd better have this back too. He'll ... Maybe he'll be feeling in need of a smoke.

BAMFORTH   Yeh ... Thanks, Jock. (*He crosses to return the cigarette case.*)

JOHNSTONE   Bamforth! Just a minute, lad.

BAMFORTH   Yeh?

JOHNSTONE   I'd like a look at that before you hand it on to him.

BAMFORTH   Ask him. Not me. It's his.

JOHNSTONE   He'll get it back. I only want it for a minute.

BAMFORTH   (*hesitates, then crosses and hands the case to* JOHNSTONE) He'd better get it back.

JOHNSTONE   He will. (*He inspects the case, slowly turning it over in his hands, then tosses it to* BAMFORTH. BAMFORTH *crosses to return it to* THE PRISONER.) Bamforth!

BAMFORTH   (*turns*) You want something else?

JOHNSTONE   No, lad. Nothing. I was just wondering, that's all.

BAMFORTH   Well?

JOHNSTONE   Are you feeling in a generous mood today?

BAMFORTH	What's that supposed to signify?
JOHNSTONE	Did you give him the case as well?
BAMFORTH	I gave him half a dozen fags, that's all. I haven't got a case myself to give away. I gave him half a dozen snouts, I've told you half a dozen times. The case belongs to him.
JOHNSTONE	Does it?
BAMFORTH	The case is his.
JOHNSTONE	That's interesting. You'd better have another shufti at it, then.
BAMFORTH	*inspects the case and is about to return it to* THE PRISONER.
MITCHEM	Pass it over, Bamforth.
BAMFORTH	What for? It's his.
MITCHEM	I'd like to once it over for myself.
BAMFORTH	(*tosses the case to* MITCHEM, *who also examines it, then turns his glance upon* THE PRISONER) All right! So it's a British case!
JOHNSTONE	Made in Birmingham.
BAMFORTH	So what? What's that supposed to prove?
MITCHEM	So tell us now how he got hold of it.
BAMFORTH	I don't know. Don't ask me.
JOHNSTONE	I bloody do! The way he got the snouts.
BAMFORTH	I gave him the fags.
JOHNSTONE	So you say.
BAMFORTH	I gave him the fags!
MITCHEM	And what about the case?
BAMFORTH	Look – I don't know. I've told you – I don't know.
EVANS	So he has been on the lifting lark? Half-inching from the boys up country.
MACLEISH	It begins to look that way.
	MACLEISH *and* EVANS *move menacingly towards* THE PRISONER.
BAMFORTH	(*planting himself between* THE PRISONER

and EVANS *and* MACLEISH) You've got it all sorted out between you.

EVANS   It stands to reason, man.

BAMFORTH   You ought to be in Scotland Yard, you lads. In Security.

MACLEISH   It's pretty obvious he's pinched the thing.

BAMFORTH   Is it?

EVANS   How else could he have got it, Bammo?

BAMFORTH   You pair of ignorant crones! Sherlock-Taffy-Bloody-Holmes and Charlie MacChan. Sexy Blake and his tartan boy assistant. How do I know where he got it from? It's you bright pair who seem to know the answers. You tell me. If I were you I'd have it cased for bloodstains and fingerprints with a magnifying glass. How does anybody cop on to a fag case? Eh? You buy them! In shops! With money! You know what money is, eh? Money, you know. The stuff they give you on a Friday night. Bits of paper. And little round rings. That's the carry-on in my home town. Where you come from they still swop things for sheep.

MACLEISH   It's a British case, Bamforth.

BAMFORTH   You're a head case, Jock. I've got a little skin and blister back in Blighty. Twelve years old. She carts around a squinting Nippo doll. Know how she got it? One night, instead of being tucked up in her little bed, she was out roaming the streets with a chopper. She knocked off nine Nippo nippers in a night nursery and nicked a golliwog, two teddy-bears and this here doll. You want to know how we found out? It's got 'Made in Japan' stamped across its pink behind. Now, work that one out.

MITCHEM   It won't wash, Bamforth. The Nips don't import fancy swag. They churn it out themselves and flog it abroad.

BAMFORTH   (*stepping aside to give* MACLEISH *and* EVANS *access to* THE PRISONER) All right! Go on. Beat him up, then. Work him over. Enjoy yourselves for once. Have a good time. Look – listen. You want to know something? You want to know who's got the biggest hoard of loot in the Far East, bar none? Who's collected more Jap swag than any regiment? I'll introduce him. (BAMFORTH *crosses to rear of hut and raises* WHITAKER'S *hand.*) On my right and stepping in the ring at six stone six – the terror of the New-castle Church Army Hostel: Private Winnie Whitaker!

WHITAKER   (*embarrassed at being drawn into the proceedings*) Cut it out, Bammo.

BAMFORTH   Take a bow, son. Here he is. The sole proprietor of the Samuel Whitaker War Museum. It's worth hard gelt in anybody's lingo.
            WHITAKER *manages to extricate his hand from* BAMFORTH'S *grip.*

MITCHEM   What are you getting at?

BAMFORTH   Ask the boy himself. He's the proud possessor. Come on, Whitaker, my old son, don't be bashful. Tell them all about your battle honours. What you did in the war, dad.

WHITAKER   I don't know what you're supposed to be talking about.

BAMFORTH   Don't you? Smudger knows. Smudger's seen it. He can bear me out.

SMITH   Leave the kid alone, Bammo. There's no harm in it.

BAMFORTH   It's true, isn't it?

SMITH   Look – lay off the lad.

BAMFORTH   Is it the truth?

SMITH   Yes ... He's got a bit of swag.

BAMFORTH   A bit! That's the bloody understatement of the war, is that.

WHITAKER   It's only souvenirs, Bammo.

EVANS   What kind of souvenirs you got, Sammy?

BAMFORTH   He's got it in his locker back at camp. Smudge and me had a shufti one morning when he left it open. Well, come on Whitto, don't be shy. Tell them what you've got.

WHITAKER	Just some odds and ends, man, and a few things I've picked up, that's all.
BAMFORTH	Tell them!
WHITAKER	Some Jap buttons and a couple of rounds.
BAMFORTH	And the rest.
WHITAKER	A Nippo cap badge and a belt.
BAMFORTH	Go on.
WHITAKER	That's all.
BAMFORTH	I've seen inside your locker.
WHITAKER	That's all there is.
BAMFORTH	You're lying, Whitaker!
WHITAKER	I'm not, man. I've not got anything else.
BAMFORTH	You're a lying get!
WHITAKER	Only some bits and pieces.
SMITH	Leave him alone, Bamforth.
BAMFORTH	His locker's loaded with Jap loot. It's like a little Tokyo inside his locker.
WHITAKER	They're only souvenirs, Bammo.
BAMFORTH	Don't give me that. There's half the emperor's arsenal and the Imperial quartermaster's stores in there. When you get home with that lot, Whitaker, you won't half give the family the bull. Will you be able to chat them up, boy, on how you won the war. The Tyneside hero. (*To* EVANS *and* MACLEISH.) And you lot want to string the fives on Tojo just because he's got a Blighty fag case. If the Nips lay hands on Whitaker they'll work it out that he's a sort of military Al Capone. Him! Whitaker! Whining Whitaker. The boy who has a nervous breakdown at the thought of Madame Butterfly. Show him a rice pudding and he gets the screaming ab-dabs. He's never even seen a Jap excepting that one there.
SMITH	Can't you leave the lad alone.
BAMFORTH	All right. I've done with him. But just for the book, Whitaker, just to put these boys here right – just tell them how you copped on to the spoils of war.

WHITAKER   I don't know. I just ... they just came into my
             possession.

BAMFORTH   Tell them how!

WHITAKER   I swopped some things for them. In the N.A.A.F.I.
             Down the U.J. Club. I swopped them for some stuff
             I had myself – with some blokes I met who'd come
             down from up country.

BAMFORTH   That's all I want to know.

WHITAKER   It's not a crime.

BAMFORTH   No. No, it's not a crime. (*Crossing downstage.*) It's
             not a crime to have a fag case either. Now, go on,
             Jock, beat up the Nip.

MACLEISH   You still haven't proved, to my satisfaction, that
             that's the way he got the case.

BAMFORTH   You try and prove it different.

MACLEISH   (*turning away from* THE PRISONER) ... Och, what's it
             matter anyway ...

MITCHEM   Evans!

EVANS   Sarge?

MITCHEM   (*tossing the cigarette case to* EVANS) You'd better give
             him this back.

EVANS   Righto.

             EVANS *gives the cigarette case to* THE PRISONER, *who
             opens it, takes out a cigarette and offers one to* EVANS,
             who hesitates and then accepts. EVANS *takes out a box
             of matches and gives* THE PRISONER *a light.*

WHITAKER   (*desiring to change the conversation*) Sergeant
             Mitchem ...

MITCHEM   What's your worry?

WHITAKER   I was wondering about the time ...

MITCHEM   Do you ever do anything else?

WHITAKER   I mean about reliefs. For Smudger and myself. It's
             well turned half-past now.

MITCHEM   I know! ... All right. Who's next for stag?

MACLEISH   (*collects his rifle and crosses to rear*) Me, for one.

MITCHEM	Take over from Ticker Whitaker before he does his nut.
WHITAKER	I only mentioned it in case it might have slipped your memory, Sarge.
MITCHEM	Tick, tick, tick! You should have been a bloody clock.
WHITAKER	(*having been relieved by* MACLEISH, *he crosses downstage*) I wasn't complaining. I thought you'd forgotten.
MITCHEM	I'm not likely to with you around. (*Points to his watch.*) If ever this packs in on me I'll wrap you around my wrist. Evans!
EVANS	Sarge?
MITCHEM	Give Smudge a break. (*Indicating* THE PRISONER.) Bamforth, you just keep an eye on him.
BAMFORTH	He's all right.
MITCHEM	Just keep an eye on him, that's all.
EVANS	(*collects his rifle and crosses towards* SMITH. *As he approaches he shoulders his rifle and carries out a 'cod' guard mounting routine with exaggerated smartness.* SMITH *obeys the orders*) Old guard ... 'shun! Stand at ... ease! 'Shun! ... Slope ... Arms! One – two – three, one – two – three, one! ...Order ... arms! One – two – three, one – two–three, one! Very good, Smudger boy. You should have joined the Guards. The sentries will now dismiss for a crafty smoke in the boiler house ... old guard – to the guard room ... Dis ...
JOHNSTONE	All right, Evans. Cut out the funny stuff.
EVANS	You see how it is, Smudger? When you try to be regimental they won't have it. O.K., boyo, you scarper. I'll take over here.
SMITH	It's all yours, Taff.
	EVANS *takes up his position at the window as* SMITH *crosses downstage.* WHITAKER *and* SMITH *prop their rifles against the wall.*

WHITAKER	Hey, Taff!
EVANS	What is it, boy?
WHITAKER	Can I have a look at your book? That one you were reading out of earlier on?
EVANS	In my small pack, Whitto.
WHITAKER	(*crossing to take magazine from* EVANS*'s pack which is on the form by* THE PRISONER) Thanks, Taffy.
BAMFORTH	(*as* WHITAKER *gives* THE PRISONER *a wide berth*) It's all right, Whitto, he won't bite you, son. (BAMFORTH *watches* WHITAKER *as he takes the magazine from the pack and settles himself on the extreme end of the form.*) You trying to improve your mind?
WHITAKER	I just wanted to pass a few minutes on. (*He flicks through the pages.*) Where's that story that Taff was telling us about? The one with the Arabs.
SMITH	It's a serial, Sammy. No good starting that.
WHITAKER	I don't mind. It's something to read.
BAMFORTH	You screw the pictures, Whitaker. No good stuffing your head up with them long words. Have a butcher's at the corset adverts on the last page.
SMITH	He's not old enough for them.
BAMFORTH	He's got to start sometime. He can't stay ignorant for ever.
WHITAKER	Who's ignorant?
BAMFORTH	You are! Ignorant as a pig. Pig-ignorant, boy, that's you.
WHITAKER	That's all you know, Bamforth.
BAMFORTH	Hark at him! The innocent abroad. The voice of experience. They lock their daughters up in Newcastle when he's on leave. Go on, Whitaker, you've never been with a bint in your life.
WHITAKER	That just shows how much you know, boy!
SMITH	Never mind him, Sammy. He's pulling your leg.
WHITAKER	He doesn't know so much himself.
BAMFORTH	Have you ever been with a woman, Whitaker?

WHITAKER	'Course I have. I was courting when I left Blighty.
BAMFORTH	I bet.
SMITH	Newcastle girl, Sammy?
WHITAKER	No, Darlington lass. I met her at a dance once when I was stationed at Catterick.
BAMFORTH	Dancing! Get him! He'll be drinking beer and playing cards for money next.
WHITAKER	It was in a church hall – the dance, I mean. One of the lads in the billet took me. That's how I met this girl.
SMITH	Got a photograph?
WHITAKER	I've got a couple back at camp.
SMITH	What's she like? Bramah, eh?
WHITAKER	She's ... well, she's sort of pretty, you know, like. Mary. That's her name. Mary Pearson. Comes up to about my shoulder and sort of yellowish hair. Works for an insurance company. In the office. Oh, she's ... she's bloody pretty, Smudge. Nothing outstanding, like – but, boy, she's pretty. We was courting for three months very nearly. I was up there doing my basic training.
SMITH	Take her out much, did you?
WHITAKER	I used to get to meet her a couple of times a week, like. Whenever I could skive off. Get the bus from camp centre into Darlington and meet her nights outside a shop. Some nights we'd go to the pictures – or dancing – or something – when I could afford it, like. I wasn't loaded them days. So most nights we'd just walk up through the park, you know. Along by the river. The middle of summer I was at Catterick. Was it hot then, boy! Oh, man ...? She's only seventeen just – is it a bit young, do you think?
SMITH	Doesn't seem to make much difference – these days.
WHITAKER	So we'd just walk along by the side of the river, like. Up as far as the bridge. Happen sit down and watch them playing bowls. Sit for ten minutes or so, get up and walk back. Just a steady stroll, you know. I

	never had much money – only my bus fare there and back sometimes – but it was ... Oh, boy! Oh, you know – we had some smashing times together me and her. I wish I was back there now, boy.
SMITH	Write to her, do you?
WHITAKER	When I get the chance. When I'm back in camp. Every day if I've got the time.
SMITH	Roll on the duration, eh!
WHITAKER	I used to hear from her twice a week. I haven't had a letter from her for over a month. Almost six weeks.
SMITH	You know how it is, Sammy. Maybe she's busy.
WHITAKER	I don't know. I'm thinking happen she's got fixed up with another bloke.
SMITH	Maybe the mail's been held up.
WHITAKER	I get plenty from my mother and the old man. I think it's another bloke she's with.
SMITH	You don't want to think like that.
WHITAKER	The letters – the writing – things she said – it was different. Towards the last one, like.
SMITH	Happen be one waiting for you when you get back tomorrow.
WHITAKER	Aye. Happen so ... I don't know. I've sort of, given up, like. Hoping, you know.
	It is early evening and the light has begun to dim. The jungle is silent and a stillness falls upon the patrol. BAMFORTH *begins to sing – quietly and with a touch of sadness.*
BAMFORTH	A handsome young private lay dying,
	At the edge of the jungle he lay.
	The Regiment gathered round him,
	To hear for the last words he'd say.
	'Take the trigger-guard out of my kidneys,
	Take the magazine out of my brain,
	Take the barrel from out of my back-bone,
	And assemble my rifle again ...'
	(*In an attempt to restore the previous mood,*

BAMFORTH *rubs the top of* THE PRISONER'S *head playfully*.) Now then, Tojo, my old flowerpot, what did you think of that? That's better than you cop on from the Tokyo geisha fillies.

EVANS   (*turning at window*) It'll not be long before it's dark now, Sarge.

MACLEISH   (*without turning from window*) It's quiet out there. It's bloody quiet.

MITCHEM   (*rising*) Time we got ready for the push then. Got packed up. Got things – sorted out.

BAMFORTH   (*having taken a swig from his water bottle, he wipes the lid and offers the bottle to* THE PRISONER) Come on, Tojo son. Get a gob of this before we go.

THE PRISONER *accepts the bottle gratefully.*

JOHNSTONE   There's no more buckshees for the Nippo, Bamforth.

THE PRISONER, *sensing the meaning from* JOHNSTONE'S *tone, returns the water bottle to* BAMFORTH *without drinking.*

BAMFORTH   (*puts down the water bottle and turns to face* JOHNSTONE) I've warned you, Johnno. Don't overstep them tapes. I'll not take any more of the patter. Is it O.K. if I give the prisoner a drink, Sarge?

MITCHEM   You heard what Corporal Johnstone said, Bamforth.

BAMFORTH   (*incredulous*) You what?

JOHNSTONE   There's no more water for the Nippo.

BAMFORTH   Like Hell there isn't. The bloke's got to drink.

MITCHEM   He's had a drink – earlier on this afternoon. I gave him one myself.

BAMFORTH   He's not a camel!

MITCHEM   I'm sorry, Bamforth. We've none to spare for him.

BAMFORTH   Sorry!

MITCHEM   We'll need every drop we've got for getting back. It's dead certain that there'll be a gang of Nips round every water hole from here to base.

BAMFORTH   So we share out what we've got.

MITCHEM   No.

BAMFORTH   He gets half of mine.

MITCHEM   No! There's none for him.

BAMFORTH   He'll have to have a drink sometime. He can't go the distance without – you've got to get him back as well. (*He waits for a reply.*) We're taking him as well!

MITCHEM   I'm sorry.

JOHNSTONE   He's stopping where he is. (*He picks up* THE PRISONER'S *bayonet from the table.*) It's cobbler's for him.

BAMFORTH   No.

MITCHEM   I've got no choice.

BAMFORTH   You said he was going back.

MITCHEM   He was – before. The circumstances are altered. The situation's changed. I can't take him along.

BAMFORTH   What's the poor get done to us?

MITCHEM   It's a war. It's something in a uniform and it's a different shade to mine.

BAMFORTH   (*positioning himself between* THE PRISONER *and* JOHNSTONE) You're not doing it, Johnno.

JOHNSTONE   You laying odds on that?

BAMFORTH   For Christ's sake!

JOHNSTONE   It's a bloody Nip.

BAMFORTH   He's a man!

JOHNSTONE   (*crossing a few paces towards* THE PRISONER) Shift yourself, Bamforth. Get out of the way.

BAMFORTH   You're not doing it.

MITCHEM   Bamforth, shift yourself.

BAMFORTH   You're a bastard, Mitchem.

MITCHEM   I wish to God I was.

BAMFORTH   You're a dirty bastard, Mitchem.

MITCHEM   As far as I'm concerned, it's all these lads or him.

BAMFORTH   It's him and me.

MITCHEM   (*crossing to join* JOHNSTONE) Get to one side. That's an order.

BAMFORTH   Stick it.

MITCHEM   For the last time, Bamforth, move over.

BAMFORTH   Try moving me.

MITCHEM   I've not got time to mess about.

BAMFORTH   So come on, Whitaker! Don't sit there, lad. Whose side you on? (WHITAKER *rises slowly from the form. For a moment it would seem that he is going to stand by* BAMFORTH, *but he crosses the room to stand beyond* MITCHEM *and* JOHNSTONE.) You've got no guts, Whitaker. You know that, boy? You've just got no guts.

WHITAKER   We've got to get back, Bammo.

BAMFORTH   You're a gutless slob!

WHITAKER   I've got to get back!

BAMFORTH   Evans. Taffy, Taff! (EVANS *turns from the window.*) Put the gun on these two, son.

EVANS   I reckon Mitch is right, you know. We couldn't get him back to camp, could we, boyo? The Nips must have a Div between the camp and us.

BAMFORTH   He's going to kill him, you nit!

EVANS   You never know about that fag case, do you, son?

BAMFORTH   What's the fag case got to do with it! ... Smudger! Smudger, now it's up to you.

SMITH   Don't ask me, Bammo. Leave me out of it.

BAMFORTH   You're in it, Smudge. You're in it up to here.

SMITH   I just take orders. I just do as I'm told. I just plod on.

BAMFORTH   The plodding on has stopped. Right here. Right here you stop and make a stand. He's got a wife and kids.

SMITH   I've got a wife and kids myself. Drop it, Bammo, it's like Mitch says – it's him or us.

BAMFORTH   Jock! ...Jock! (MACLEISH *continues to stare out of the window.*) Macleish! ... (MACLEISH *does not move.*) I hope they carve your brother up. Get that? I hope they carve your bloody brother up!

MITCHEM   All right, Bamforth, you've had your say. Now shift.

BAMFORTH Shift me! Come on, heroes, shift me!

MITCHEM Whitaker! Grab a gun and cover the Nip.

BAMFORTH Don't do it, Whitaker. Stay out of it.

MITCHEM Whitaker!

WHITAKER *picks up a sten from the table and crosses to cover* THE PRISONER, *who has realized the implications and is trembling with fear.* MITCHEM *and* JOHNSTONE *move forward to overpower* BAMFORTH. JOHNSTONE *drops the bayonet on the floor and, together with* MITCHEM, *grapples with* BAMFORTH. *As they fight* THE PRISONER *begins to rise to his feet.*

WHITAKER (*already in a state of fear himself*) Get down! ... Sit down! ... (THE PRISONER *continues to rise.*) Sit down, you stupid man, or I'll have to put a bullet into you ... THE PRISONER *is standing upright as* WHITAKER'S *finger tightens on the trigger. A long burst from the sten shudders the hut and the bullets slam home into the body of* THE PRISONER *like hammer blows* THE PRISONER *doubles up and falls to the floor. The fight stops. There is a pause.* WHITAKER *drops the sten and buries his face in his hands.*) God ... God ... God ... (*His voice swells.*) Oh, God!

MITCHEM Well, that should roust out every Nip from here to Tokyo. You've made a mess of that, lad. (WHITAKER, *uncomprehending, looks at his hands.* MITCHEM *seizes him by the shoulders and shakes him savagely.*) Come on, come on! Come out of it! He's just the first.

BAMFORTH You've got the biggest souvenir of all. You've done it this time, Whitaker. Take that and hang it on the front room wall ...

BAMFORTH'S *words are cut short as* MITCHEM *strikes him across the face.*

MITCHEM We've had enough from you.

EVANS *and* MACLEISH *have left their posts and, together with* SMITH, *are drawn in fascination towards the body of* THE PRISONER.

JOHNSTONE   All right. Get back. It's just a corpse. You'll see a whole lot more like that before you've done.

MITCHEM   Right. All of you. We're moving out. In double time. Get your gear together. Thirty seconds and we're off. Any longer and this place will be rotten with Nips. Any man not ready stays behind. Move!
The members of the patrol put on their packs, ammunition pouches, etc.

MITCHEM   Johnno, ditch your stuff. Can you work the set? (JOHNSTONE *nods assent and crosses to radio.*) Give it one last crack. (JOHNSTONE *switches on the set and the crackle of interference grows behind.*) We haven't got a snowball's chance in Hell of getting back. So try and let them know the Japs have broken through.

JOHNSTONE   (*nods and switches to 'transmit'*) Blue Patrol calling Red Leader ... Blue Patrol calling Red Leader ... Are you receiving me ... Are you receiving me... Come in Red Leader ... Over ... (JOHNSTONE *switches to 'receive' and the interference swells.*) Not a rotten peep.

MITCHEM   All right. Jack it in.

JOHNSTONE   (*rips off headphones, leaving the set switched on. He straps on his ammunition pouches and picks up the sten from the floor.*) Let's have you then! We're pushing off!

MITCHEM   (*picking up his own sten*) Leave what you haven't got. And move!
The members of the patrol collect their rifles and cross to the door. JOHNSTONE *glances out of the window.*

JOHNSTONE   All clear.

MITCHEM   (*opens the door*) I'll break the trail. Johnno, you bring up the rear. (JOHNSTONE *nods.*) All right, let's go.
One by one the members of the patrol follow MITCHEM *through the door.* JOHNSTONE *is the last to leave. As the door closes behind* JOHNSTONE *the interference increases on the set and suddenly it bursts into life.*

OPERATOR   (*on distort*) ... Red Leader calling Blue Patrol ... Red

Leader calling Blue Patrol ... Come in Blue Patrol ...
Over ...

*A machine-gun chatters in the jungle and is joined by
another. we hear the sound of one or two rifles and
the screams of dying men. The noise of gunfire fades
away to leave only the whimper of one wounded man
– it is* WHITAKER. *The door is pushed open and*
JOHNSTONE *enters. He has a bullet wound in his side
and the blood is seeping through his shirt. Slamming
the door shut, he leans upon it to regain his breath.*

WHITAKER   (*screams out from the jungle in fear*) God! ... God! ...
(*A final cry of terror louder than any we have heard
previously.*) Mother ... !

We hear the sound of a single shot and WHITAKER *is
dead.* JOHNSTONE *presses his hand to his side. The set
splutters into life again.*

OPERATOR   (*on distort*) ... Are you receiving me, Blue Patrol? ...
Are you receiving me? ... Over ...

JOHNSTONE   (*crosses slowly to the set, picks up hand-set and
switches to 'transmit'*) Get knotted! All of you! You
hear? The whole damn lot of you!

*JOHNSTONE switches off the set and crosses towards the
body of* THE PRISONER. *As he passes the window there is
a short burst of machine-gun fire. He ducks below
window level. Squatting by the side of the body, he
takes the cigarette case from* THE PRISONER'S *pocket and
helps himself to a cigarette. Sticking the cigarette in
his mouth, he returns the case to* THE PRISONER'S
*pocket. He tugs the white silk scarf, now spattered
with blood, from* THE PRISONER'S *neck and crawls
across to beneath the window, where he ties the scarf
round the barrel of his sten. It has all required a great
effort, and he lights the cigarette and inhales deeply
before continuing. Squatting below the window, he
waves the white flag and, in turn, takes long pulls at
the cigarette. For a moment there is complete silence
and then a bird sings out in the jungle.*

THE CURTAIN FALLS

QUESTIONS AND EXPLORATIONS

1 Keeping Track

The questions in this section are designed to help your understanding of the play. They may be used as you read the play or afterwards for discussion.

Act One

1 What do the stage directions tell you about the setting of the play?

2 Why do the soldiers enter the hut so cautiously?

3 What is the men's reaction when they find the hut deserted?

4 Mitchem orders two men to go on 'stag' or sentry duty. Why?

5 What seems to be the relationship between the Corporal, Johnstone, and one of the privates, Bamforth?

6 What is the state of the radio set?

7 What instructions does Mitchem give to the rest of the men about the way they should spend the next half hour?

8 Why do you think Mitchem suggests that he and Johnstone should take a look outside the hut?

9 What does Bamforth threaten to do to Johnstone if he should meet him after the war?

10 Smith intervenes in the discussion between Bamforth and Evans. Why?

11 Macleish does the same a few minutes later. What is his reason?

12 Macleish explains why he is supporting army discipline. How does Bamforth tease him about this?

13 After annoying Smith and then Macleish, Bamforth's fooling about then affects Whitaker. Why does he want Bamforth to be quiet?

14 What is Bamforth's reaction when Whitaker insists he heard something on the radio?

15 Why do you think Evans needs the magazine *Ladies' Companion and Home?* What confuses him about trying to follow the serial?

16 Read Bamforth's speech on page 14 beginning 'Eighteen months! Stroll on!' From this, what do you gather is Bamforth's opinion of the girls back in England?

17 Evans involves Smith in the conversation. Describe Smith's home life and family.

18 Why do Bamforth and Evans start to fight?

19 Why does Whitaker interrupt them? What happens?

20 The men are clearly all frightened in case they are captured by the Japanese. What is Bamforth's plan of escape? Do you take him seriously?

21 On pages 20 and 21, Bamforth makes two long speeches. How do they annoy first Whitaker and then Macleish? What is the result?

22 What are the various ways in which Smith tries to stop the fight between Bamforth and Macleish? What does stop it?

23 What is Mitchem's reaction to the fight? How does he restore order?

24 Why do you think Macleish refuses to name the man who had annoyed him? Why does Bamforth own up?

25 On page 26, Sergeant Mitchem gives Bamforth a long lecture. What does he tell him?

26 Mitchem outlines the situation to his men and describes their intended journey back to base. Why does Macleish question him?

27 What worries Johnstone about the possibility of something coming through on the radio set? How does Mitchem try to reassure him?

28 When Whitaker eventually does hear something on the set, how does the playwright build up the tension both for the characters in the play and for the audience in the theatre?

29 Whitaker and Mitchem are the first two to realise the implications of hearing Japanese voices. What are the implications?

30 What is Macleish's reaction to the realisation that the Japanese army is obviously very near?

31 On page 32, Mitchem sums up their present situation and alters his plans for their evacuation. Why?

32 What does Bamforth see which changes their plans radically?

33 Why does the Japanese soldier come into the hut?

34 Why does Mitchem dart out of the door?

35 Why is it that Evans cannot kill the Japanese soldier with his bayonet?

36 How does Mitchem speak to the prisoner? Why is this, do you think?

37 How does Bamforth treat the prisoner at first?

38 For what reason does Mitchem want to take the prisoner back to the British Camp alive?

39 What is Johnstone's attitude towards the prisoner? Give two examples of his behaviour to support your view.

40 How does the Japanese soldier try to communicate and even try to be friendly with his captors?

41 What is Johnstone's reaction when Bamforth gives the prisoner a cigarette?

42 How does Bamforth take advantage of this?

43 What is Mitchem's reaction? How does he punish Bamforth?

44 What news is brought by Smith and Macleish? How does this news change their plans? What will now happen to the prisoner?

45 When the radio set transmits we all – the characters and the audience – hear the voice of the Japanese radio signaller. What effect does this message have on the British soldiers, the Japanese prisoner and on you, the audience?

Act Two

1 How do we know that Whitaker is jumpy and nervous? Give two examples.

2 What do you think is the point of the story about Whitaker and his watch?

3 Why is Macleish so keen to convince himself that the Japanese prisoner 'doesn't seem a bad sort of bloke'?

4 What is Mitchem's theory about a man's ability to kill another man?

5 What does Mitchem's long speech on page 56 tell you about his relationship with women?

6 Why is Macleish so slow in realising, or admitting to himself, that Mitchem intends to kill the Japanese prisoner?

7 How does Mitchem justify his decision?

8 What is Macleish's reaction to this and how does Mitchem again justify his intention of killing the prisoner?

9 Why do you think Johnstone volunteers to do the killing?

10 The prisoner gives Macleish a cigarette which turns out to be British. How does this make the men suspicious of him?

11 Johnstone tears up the prisoner's photographs of this family. What does this tell you about him?

12 What is the truth about the prisoner and the cigarettes? The cigarette case is a different matter. How does Bamforth attempt to explain this?

13 We next learn about Whitaker's collection of Japanese souvenirs. What does this tell us about him?

14 How does Bamforth use this story to explain the prisoner's possession of the cigarette case?

15 How do they tease Whitaker? As a result Whitaker tells the story of his girlfriend back in England. What impression do we get of him from this?

16 Mitchem refuses to allow Bamforth to give the prisoner a drink. Why? What does this incident tell us?

17 Bamforth tries to protect the prisoner against Johnstone and then against Mitchem. How does this action affect the rest of the patrol?

18 What does the prisoner do that causes Whitaker to pull the trigger on the sten-gun?

19 Mitchem realises the effect the noise of the firing will have on their chances of survival. How does he react?

20 When Johnstone tries to use the radio to warn base camp, the radio appears to be dead but when all the men have left the hut the audience hears a message

from the British radio operator. Why does the
playwright do this?

21 Johnstone staggers back into the hut, wounded, and
then raises a white flag in surrender. Why is it ironic
that it should be Johnstone who is to be taken prisoner
by the Japanese?

2 Explorations

The questions in this section are more detailed and rely on
your having read the whole play. Many lend themselves to
either oral or written responses.

A Characters

Mitchem

1 Imagine you are one of the other men in this play.
What would be your opinion of the way that Mitchem
has led the patrol? Write a letter home in which you say
what you think of Mitchem. Is he a good leader? Is he
professional? Are you willing to follow his instructions
unquestioningly?

Johnstone

2 What qualities in Johnstone do you think might have
persuaded his superiors to promote him?

3 What do you think the men serving under Johnstone
think of him?

4 What do you think of Johnstone? Do you like or
dislike him? Why?

Bamforth

5 Bamforth is clearly a trouble-maker and a nuisance to
Mitchem and Johnstone but he has a side to his
personality which redeems him in our eyes – his

compassion for the prisoner. Does your attitude towards Bamforth change during the play? How do you feel about him at the end?

6 Why do you think Bamforth defends the prisoner in the way that he does? Does his defence come from anger at authority or from a genuine concern for the prisoner?

7 Imagine Bamforth lives at the end of the play. Write his diary entry explaining his motivation for defending the prisoner.

Macleish

8 In the long conversation which Macleish and Mitchem have about the fate of the Japanese soldier, we learn a great deal about Macleish. How would you sum up his personality at the end of the play? Do you like or dislike him?

Whitaker

9 Whitaker is the most frightened and inexperienced member of the patrol. To an extent the tragedy comes about because of the broken radio and his incompetence which causes the prisoner to be shot. How would you defend him?

Evans

10 From his relationship with Bamforth and from what we learn about his girlfriend and his reading of his mother's women's magazines, what impression do you get of Evans? Is he important or interesting?

Smith

11 We hear during the play of Smith's wife and family and his home life. He also tries to smooth the tension and protect Whitaker from criticism. What kind of man is he?

The Japanese Soldier

12 This is a difficult part to play because the Japanese soldier says nothing, having to communicate through body movements and reactions to the others. Imagine that you are this prisoner and survive at the end. How would you describe your ordeal? What are your impressions of the British soldiers?

General

13 Imagine that the patrol does live through these events and manages to slip through the Japanese patrols back to their base. Choose any two characters and write out their reports of the events in the hut. Try to choose two contrasting views if you can.

B Themes

1 The playwright, Willis Hall, has said that the play 'is about human dignity'. Discuss which of the characters, in your opinion, retains his dignity and which does not.

2 Although *The Long and the Short and the Tall* is about a particular war, the British and the Japanese in Malaya in 1942, it has been staged about other wars. Why do you think the play has such universal appeal?

3 The characters in this play are in a frightening situation. In what ways does being frightened alter the way in which they behave and react?

4 Throughout the play we are aware of the patrol's faulty radio. Imagine you are the radio operator back at the British base and have managed to understand some of what has been happening. Write the report for your C.O. of what you have gathered.

5 If you could interview the playwright, Willis Hall, about his play either for a newspaper article or for the television, what would you choose to ask him?

C In Performance

1 You are the director of this play. Write out ten points you would give as advice to the two actors playing Mitchem and Bamforth. Think about what aspects of each character you would need to highlight in performance. How might the actors use voice, gesture and movement to achieve this?

2 Look again at the end of Act One and the beginning of Act Two. Construct the dialogue and happenings which you think might have been going on while you and the rest of the audience were enjoying the interval in the play.

3 The play is in two acts. Write a third act in which a Japanese patrol enters the hut and finds Johnstone wounded and holding a white flag of surrender.

4 If you were asked to act in this play, which part would appeal particularly to you?

5 Design a poster advertising a production of the play for your local theatre. How will you interest and attract a potential audience? What other publicity would you require in order to make the play a success? What form would this take?

Glossary

(Meanings are given with reference to use on the pages shown)

Ab-dabs	usually *screaming* 21, 44: hysterical fit, 75: bowel upset
Al Capone	75: American gangster
Barrack-room lawyer	26: man who makes trouble by insisting on legal rights
Batt.	28: battery
Bints	6: girls
Blighty	14, 25, 52, 56, 66, 69, 73, 75, 79, 79: England, English (from Hindustani bilayati)
Blocks	put the blocks on 48: stop
Bog	8: latrine
Bonce	40: head
Book	26, 60: rigid adherence to what is legal, i.e. in the book of King's Regulations
Bramah	79: gorgeously beautiful (from Hindu deity, whose idols were so)
Buckshee	81: gift, 32: free, hence worthless (from Persian word for present)
Bull	15, 55, 57, 69, 75: nonsense, empty talk
Bundle, go a bundle on	20, 56, 70: be wildly enthusiastic about or stake everything on, make a bold bid
Bungy	18: food
Butcher's	78: look (rhyming slang, *butcher's hook*)

Butterfly, *Madame*	75: i.e. anything Japanese (Madame Butterfly is the Japanese heroine of Puccini's opera of that name)
Call out *the time*	21, 32, 46: talk loudly and confidently, 21: give orders
Cap and *belt off*	22: military practice of taking off a soldier's hat and belt before parading him for disciplinary sentence
Carve up (v)	5: beat up, 83: kill, (n), 14: swindle
Case (v)	73: examine
Charlie *McChan*	73: Charlie Chan was a detective in a series of films. *A Charlie* (56) is a fool (possibly from Charlie Chaplin)
Chuff	29: disregard, 32: curse
Civvy street	5: civilian life
Cobbler's	82: end (in Australia the last sheep to be sheared is called the cobbler's – originally perhaps the *cobbler's last*)
Cod	20, 77: mock
Come	assert, insist on, 23: *Come the regimental,* 10: insist on procedure according to King's Regulations. Come the hard stuff, 25: try to appear tough. *Come his rank:* assert his authority. *Come the greater glory of mankind,* 60: claim to care greatly about ideals. *Comes the ab-dabs,* 44: goes beserk
Come it on	5, 21, 25, 26, 40, 43: behave provocatively, ask for trouble
Compo	4: composition pack containing rations for one day
Connor	66: food (from Urdu *Khana*)

Conshi	60: conscientious objector to fighting
Cop	37, 39, 57, 61: Get, take. *Cop on to, cop on for, cop on* 40, 43, 56, 61, 73, 75: get, accept, get position of, get involved with. *No cop* 57: no use
Creamer	14: mug (rhyming slang – cream-jug)
Creek	31, 32, 41: *up the creek without a paddle:* 3, 13: in difficulties (from navy slang – away from anchorage)
Crumb (n)	32: contemptible person; (adj), 18: contemptible (also crummy)
Dancers	56: stairs
Detail	18, 43: partly detailed or ordered to do a particular duty
Dinky-doo, number-two	45: rhyme for 2 in games like Housie-housie (in Australia dinkum means good)
Dis	3, 9, 28: out of order (especially of radio equipment)
Div.	83: division, military unit organized under single command and capable of operating independently. An infantry division would include roughly 12,000 men
Do, do in, or do for	36, 42, 59, 60: kill
Doolally	9: weak defective (from Deolali, mental hospital in India)
Dracula	55: bloodsucking monster, familiar in horror films
Drag	4, 34: brief smoke
Drop (you) one on	7, 70 : hit (you)

Drum	15: house, lodging
Duff	29: useless, defective
Fives	75: fists
Fix (n), get a fix on	49: locate, get indication of position (service jargon)
Fred Karno's mob	10, 31: Fred Karno was a pre-1914 comedian, whose performance depicted imbecile incompetence: a wryly satirical soldiers' song of the 1914–18 war began: 'We are Fred Karno's army'
Geisha girls	30, *Geisha fillies* 81: Japanese dancing-girls
Gelt	74: money (from German *geld*)
Geneva Convention	39: International agreement of 1906 regulating treatment of prisoners of war
Get (n)	22, 34, 40, 75, 82: person, wretch (coarse or abusive term)
Get fell in	23: order to stand in drill formation (consciously rough and ungrammatical language)
Gillo	2: move quickly
Ginks	32: men (coarse term)
Give us the heels together	10: order to stand at attention
Gob	53, 81: drink (*Gob* is originally a dialect word for *mouth*)
Graft	48: hard work
Gripe	32: complain
Haggis	20: peculiarly Scottish dish. Bamforth pulls a Scotsman's leg about haggis, and a Welshman's about leeks or Eisteddfods, in a

sort of pointless badinage

Haircut to breakfast time	5: i.e. at all hours – one version of a phrase commonly used in the Services
Half-inch	52, 72: steal (rhyming with pinch)
Happen	54, 57, 61, 65, 67, 70, 79, 80: perhaps (from Northern dialect)
Hard case	25, 26: tough, aggressive person
Harry	32, 53, 56, 59: name used disparagingly. Harry Tate was a comedian, and Harry Tate's army was similar to Fred Karno's mob
Herb	67: man
How's your father?	14: music-hall catchphrase, here used without precise meaning but with indefinable comic suggestion, cf., Haircut to breakfast time
Hump (n)	36, 70: effort, force, blow. (v), 18: carry. Gets my hump 67: annoys. Humpy 4: load
i.c.	4, 9, 10: in charge
Jack it in	5, 38, 45, 70, 85: stop it, give it up, 54: abandon fighting
Jack the Ripper	37: 19th century murderer
Joskins	32: very raw recruits
Joy	28: success, satisfaction
Judies	14, 56: girls
Kick-off	13: start
King's Regs	23, 26: King's Regulations lay down the soldier's duties, rights and procedures. *To come King's Regs* is to insist on legal rights or obligations
Kip	4, 29: sleep

Knock off	17: stop; 43: kill; 52: steal
Knotted, *Get knotted*	20, 86: coarse insult (The offensiveness depends on context, not meaning)
Kybosh, put the	48: stop, thwart
Lacas	2: anglicized versions of Malay word lêcas meaning *hurry up!*
Looey	11: lieutenant
Meal, Don't *make a meal* *out of it*	41: don't overdo it
Mob	18, 25, 27, 48, 59: military unit
Mockers	39; put the mockers on (cockney): put the evil eye on, i.e. kill
Mouth	2: insolence; big with the mouth 25: talking aggressively; shoot of your mouth 31: talk big
Muckers	44: pals (men who *muck in together*)
Mugs away	56: phrase used in the game of darts, meaning that the losers of the last game are to start the next. Mitchem puns on this special sense of 'mugs' and the more common meaning (dupes or simpletons)
N.A.A.F.I.	18, 52, 76: canteen run by Navy, Army and Air Forces Institutes
Nick (n)	3: prison; (v) 73: steal
Nip, Nippo	20, 23, 27, 32 *et passim:* Japanese
Nub	35: cigarette end; 68 cigarette
Nut, do his nut	8, 32: get excited or angry; 61: go beserk
Nut, put in the	5: butt an opponent with the head
Once over	72: look at

Orders	32: *warning you for C.O.'s orders:* threatening to bring you before the Commanding Officer for breach of discipline
P.B.I.	19: poor bloody infantry
Press, up to	34: up to the present moment
Pull	69: assert, plead, use influence of, pull his rank, 6, pull the tape, 21
Put him one on	23: aim a blow at him
Rising Sun	20: emblem of Japan
Rita Hayworth	38: film star
Roll on	29, 53; Rollon the Duration 80: was a common expression of exasperation with the war, a wry appeal for the end of it
Rookie	xxi, xxii: raw beginner (apparently from recruit)
R.S.M.	53: Regimental Sergeant-Major, responsible for discipline
Sarge	4, 27, 28, *et passim:* abbreviation of *sergeant* as form of address, familiar or even friendly in tone
Sarnt	24, 25, 26, *et passim;* smart, soldierly form of *sergeant,* intended to be respectful or mock-respectful
Saw you coming, they	51: they realized you were easily duped
Say that again, you can	61: too true! Glum or ironic exclamation of agreement
Scarper	19, 77: abound, escape (Italian scappare. Also punning association with rhyming slang, Scapa Flow for go)

Screaming ab-dabs:	see *ab-dabs*
Screw	78: same idea as *chuff,* but ruder
Sew up	48: deal with a problem
Shouting the odds	6: talking loudly and importantly
Shufti	66, 72, 74: look (from Arabic)
Skin and blister	73: rhyming slang for *sister*
Skive	26, 34: escape duty
Slot	70: stab
Snappers	15, 45: children
Snout	69, 72: cigarette
S.O.B.	28: son of a bitch (American insult)
Sort out	5, 22: quarrel by fighting; 14: deal with 81: organize
Spout	31: breech (of rifles)
Stag	2, 3, 27, 39, 76: sentry duty
Stick	19, 67, 83: treat contemptuously, dispose of
Stick, make it	46: sustain, get (e.g. a charge) proved and acted on
Stipes, three	26: chevron of sergeant's rank
Stroll on	11, 14, 18, 19, 21, 31, 45: variant of *roll on,* q.v.
Swallow	35: short smoke
Tapes	5, 7, 10, 21, 22, 60, 61: N.C.O.'s stripes indicating rank. *Over-step them tapes* 81: exceed your authority
Tick	27, 77: complaint

Tod, on one's	12, 20, 34, 35: alone (from rhyming slang: on his *Tod Sloan, on his own*)
Toe-rag	5: dispicable person who licks the sergeant's boots
Tojo	20, 30, 37, 40, 42, 43 et passim: Japanese Prime Minister, 1941–44
Tripes	24: entrails
Two's up	11, 12: (I'm) next in turn
u/s	3, 28: unserviceable, out of order
U.J. club	76: Union Jack club for servicemen
Valentino Rudolph	57: (1895–1926) star of silent films, famous for 'handsome lover' roles
W.O.Is	xxi: Warrant Officers, first class
Work over	73: beat up
Yellow peril	21: supposed threat from Japanese (or Chinese)
Yob	61: lout (blackslang for *boy*)